THE FEEL-GOOD EXPERIENCE

THE FEEL-GOOD EXPERIENCE

Growing Your Physical Therapy Practice
with 5-Star Customer Service

Steven L. Line, PT, OCS, ATC

Sheldonville Publishing ▪ Columbus, Nebraska ▪ 2021

The Feel-Good Experience:
Growing Your Physical Therapy Practice with 5-Star Customer Service

by Steven L. Line, PT, OCS, ATC

Published by
Sheldonville Publishing
3211 25th Street
Columbus, Nebraska 68601

ISBN: 978-1-7370536-0-6 trade paperback
        978-1-7370536-1-3 electronic book

First printing

MANUFACTURED IN THE UNITED STATES OF AMERICA

This book is dedicated to my wife, Kristine, and my business partner, Rusty, for believing and supporting the vision of TFGE and taking on the personal mission to ensure that it was implemented daily.

Contents

Foreword

Growing a physical therapy business is no easy task.

When you and I graduated physical therapy school, we likely hung on "high quality of care and word-of-mouth referrals" as our personal mantra for career trajectory and practice growth.

Those two concepts are common.

Unfortunately, if you have any experience in the real world, you quickly realize that success in PT is more than quality of care and word of mouth referrals.

We have all worked with the physical therapist who had 23 letters after their name and poor patient rapport. We've also likely worked with the physical therapist who had fair clinical skills and was amazing with people.

In the end, who do you think helps more people?

If you're reading this book, *The Feel-Good Experience*, I'm going to assume you're a private practice owner—or at least an aspiring one. You're likely wanting to learn from others who have accomplished what you want to accomplish. You don't want to reinvent the wheel. You want to avoid the pitfalls. You're looking for the best information to build the most effective systems and improve your part of the world through physical therapy.

That's smart.

If that's the case, here's why I believe this book is worth your time.

Let's start with the author, Steve Line. When I hear the word *integrity*, Steve is the person I think of. Steve and I first met at a Breakthrough event a few years ago. We both are looking to continue to grow our practices in spite of the rapidly changing healthcare environment.

We have a nearly parallel business history in private practice: Steve and his team helping people through physical therapy in Columbus, Nebraska; my team and me working to do the same here in Harrisburg, Pennsylvania. We've shared many of the same struggles, wins, cognitions, realizations, and *aha* moments over time.

As is often said, most overnight successes are 20 years in the making.

Steve has put that time in.

During the early days of the pandemic (try to remember what it was like three months into the national health emergency, the peak of the shutdown), Steve and his team at Columbus PT hit all-time highs for visits. How was that possible?

The key ingredient to achieving that growth was the system Steve outlines for you here.

He not only has the experience but he organized his system and shares it with you here in a way that you can apply it and be more effective as a clinician and businessperson.

Is This the Right System?

Are you the type of owner who wants to attract the right team and put effective systems in place?

Do you want your team aligned on a long term vision to improve the physical therapy care in your area?

If you answered yes to these questions, then Steve's TFGE system is for you.

A Few Takeaways

1. The four skills pyramid. Simple and easy to understand. We're sharing this with all of our clinical directors and team members.

2. The flashlight concept. My wife and I talked about this last night—literally. It's a universal principle we all need to understand when interacting with other people.

3. Mints at the front desk. This is one of the many things Steve shared in this book that we had never personally discussed before, but for good reasons both of us do it.

The best books are ones that help improve your thinking for the long term. I believe this is one of those books.

I hope *The Feel-Good Experience* helps you on your private practice journey.

Chad Madden, physical therapist,
founder of Madden & Gilbert Physical Therapy,
cofounder of Breakthrough

Harrisburg, Pennsylvania
May 2021

Acknowledgments

My dream to be a published author began in 1979 as a starry-eyed first grader with an enormous imagination. Multiple unpublished works passed through Big Chief tablets and spiral notebooks over the years, until 2006, when The Feel-Good Experience was spiritually breathed into me.

Without the guidance, patience, and professionalism of several people, my first published work wouldn't have been possible.

Thanks first and foremost to the team of Columbus Physical Therapy, P.C., of past and present, who believed and supported the mission of The Feel-Good Experience and gave me the confidence to fulfill my vision.

Thanks to Chandler Bolt and the staff of Self-Publishing School for removing my apprehension, giving me tools to publish a book, and providing a community of similar amateur authors to collaborate.

Thanks to Qat Wanders and Christina Bagni of Wandering Words Media for their initial editing, taking fifteen years' worth of writings, data, and notes and compiling them into a beginning framework of an actual book.

Thanks to Rachel Williams of SPS for her willingness to listen to my intuition about the feel of my book and for taking her personal time to review it and give me some honest feedback. Her kindness and professionalism were perfectly timed in this process.

Thanks to Katie Chambers of Beacon Point LLC for her amazing final-level editing. I have said it before and I will say it again, I would trust her with my family. That is how much I believe in her skills and talents and how much I trust her instincts with composition. She affected me as an author and restored my belief in my ability to publish this book.

Finally, I want to thank my Lord and Savior, Jesus Christ, for creating me with the gift of writing and creation. To you, be all the glory, honor, and praise!

THE FEEL-GOOD EXPERIENCE

Introduction

Proximo: "Listen to me. Learn from me. I was the best because the crowd loved me. Win the crowd. And you will win your freedom."
Maximus: "I will win the crowd. I will give them something they have never seen before."
—*Gladiator*, Universal Pictures, 2000

The inspiration for **The Feel-Good Experience** came in 2006, during a time of intense emotional pressure for my company and me. We had tremendous turmoil, internally and externally, with employee challenges and competitor pressures. Seven years had passed since I founded the company and we were growing, but that growth had stalled, and we suddenly found ourselves in a free fall.

We got good patient outcomes, but physicians and other referral sources still weren't supporting us. In fact, many of our patients' doctors told them to go to the competition even after they demanded to return to us for care. The problem was we lacked an identity and individuality that differentiated us from the competition. Regardless of the raving patient reviews and all our hard work over the years, we still were no different than any other physical therapist's (PT) practice around. We had become "vanilla."

We had to do something that created independence from the politics of community popularity and physician controls dictating patient choices. The famous line from the movie *Gladiator*, "Win the crowd, and you'll win your freedom," kept resonating with me. I thought if we kept trying to compete with the other PT practices in our town that had community connections and had been here longer, we will not survive.

However, if we can win the crowd, the patient, the consumer, and the general public in every interaction we have with them and leave a positive feeling with them at every turn, we have a greater chance of getting patients and of getting results! They will return for their next appointment and look forward to coming in to see us. Furthermore, if we can impact them emotionally, the next time they need care they will choose us again—and they will certainly not hesitate to refer friends and family to us.

Despite this truth, healthcare industry models have historically focused solely on the clinician's skillset. Traditional clinics lack warmth, connection, relationship, positive psychology, and of course, customer service. Our practice challenges were many, but all could be resolved if we were willing to shed the old ways of thinking and move toward systematic service models that hotels, restaurants, and every other business in the world already operated from. If we could take a stiff, cold, scientific institutional model and inject LIFE into it, taking a page from the hospitality industry, we not only could survive as a business but we would also *transform* the profession and its standards.

No longer would we pour our energy into our weaknesses, remaining dependent solely upon a single therapist's clinical skill. Instead, we would redirect and reengineer a system that is simple, repeatable, and sustainable. Just as two heads are better than one, a team-oriented approach is better than a solo approach. A team-oriented approach captures all the personalities, traits, talents, gifts, and expertise into one deliverable service experience: The Feel-Good Experience!

While you can find a lot of customer service models in use today that provide good service, you would have to read a thousand different books on as many different topics to capture everything that is rolled into *The Feel-Good Experience*. It is the *only* model out there that incorporates nearly every aspect of consumer principles, as well as behavioral psychology, emotional intelligence communication, presentation, business, finance, leadership, attitude, altruism, trust, teamwork, efficacy, efficiency, business results, and ultimately, patient improvement physically, emotionally, mentally, and spiritually. It leaves no stone unturned when it comes to the mysteries of human beings and their reactions to certain stimuli as it pertains to consumer satisfaction!

Benefits

The benefits of studying and implementing The Feel-Good Experience are many. You will gain greater confidence in yourself and will draw closer together as a team, delivering service and attaining results with the consumer. You will have greater job satisfaction because you will have more success with less effort. You will work smarter, not harder. If you are a PT clinic owner, clinic director, or department head, you will find great value in turning every interaction into an opportunity to expand your business, promote your service, and increase your profits.

But don't take my word for it. The proof of this system's effectiveness is in our results. Since the creation of The Feel-Good Experience, our company has grown *thirty-five times larger* and has received our region's prestigious "Best Physical Therapist Clinic" award eleven out of the past fourteen years, including nine years in a row. If you follow this simple system, you can achieve these results, too.

Chapter 1

The Nuts and Bolts

The Feel-Good Experience (TFGE) system considers not only the patient's obvious physical needs to be addressed with physical therapy but also addresses the patient's needs, wants, and feelings about their care. To retain a current customer and build a customer for life, we must create an amazing experience—versus simply completing a business transaction.

When was the last time you walked out of the post office whistling and in a great mood because you were touched so deeply? If you did whistle a tune on your way out of the post office, it was because of how you were treated by the staff inside. The quality of your experience when mailing a package depends whether your package was delivered correctly and if you were treated with a personal connection. Even the post office can use TFGE!

It is that deep, intimate service connection that gives us a happy, satisfied feeling. In fact, that is exactly what happens when someone describes the feeling of falling in love. Granted, we may not be falling in love with our physical therapy provider, yet TFGE is all about trying to recreate the same uniqueness, emotions, and satisfying experience.

Whether it's falling in love or having a great physical therapy appointment, it is those primal experiences that imprint on a person's psyche. If a patient has positive feelings about each encounter they have in PT, don't you think they will want to return for their next appointment—or come back in the future if more care is needed?

Core Concepts

The topic of "value-added customer service" is particularly foreign in healthcare. The uniqueness of this model can be better understood with clarity of the following terms.

Self-Limiting Beliefs

Our beliefs are what determine our attitudes and opinions. Beliefs can be supporting and strengthening as well as limiting when viewed in a narrow scope. Healthcare, since the twentieth century, has evolved into an ego- or self-centered service delivered in an exceedingly more mechanical and less relational manner. Health care costs, declining provider reimbursements, and overwhelmed providers have created a decline in patient connection. Yet, it is this relationship that creates added value for the customer. Evidence-based practices, treatment paradigms that restrict a physical therapist's sessions to one of strictly following the science, remove some of the greatest aspects of treatment, mainly empathy and trust.

Five minutes spent listening to a patient tell their personal history of back pain is far more value-added than five minutes of telling them all about the biomechanics of the lumbar spine. Scientific discussions referred to as "patient education" only makes the physical therapist feel better about themselves and their knowledge, but does little for the patient's condition. Providers who tend to be strong advocates for "tech over touch" can miss a grand opportunity to help their patients. Ethos, our beliefs, values, and principles, guide us in our endeavors, but our perspective can be limited if not judged in the proper context. Learning people skills, such as communication, influence, and leadership, will yield greater patient satisfaction than merely treatment skills alone.

A "SERVE-ant" Leadership Model

Customer service departments exist to handle dissatisfaction or poor customer service. Simply put, you are in line at a customer service counter because your experience was incomplete. TFGE is about changing our mindset toward how we view the concept of customer service.

The word "service" literally means "to serve" or perform an "act of assistance" for someone.[1]

Therefore, customer service is an act of assistance to the customer, or to "serve the customer."

Expanding the premise further, one who "serves" has the title of "servant." Thus, **in order to deliver The Feel-Good Experience correctly, one has to take on a "servant mindset."** The opportunity to serve people is a true gift and a selfless act. The act of service is not one of weakness but of power, due to your choice whether to accept this mindset. When you *choose* to be a servant and desire to give great service, you are not a lowly peasant, downtrodden and suppressed by a haughty customer, but instead are a "servant leader" who chooses the humble act of service to another human and, thus, is empowered. From this position, you can lead and emulate behavior vs. ordering and commanding to create change.

Necessity of Skilled Care

A core concept is to be ethical in your practice. "Would this patient decline without therapy, or would they honestly be able to get this product at home?" This is a key ethical question we install within our service system that enforces checks and balances on the customer/business side of the scale. It ensures our product is of the highest ethical and technical quality possible. We always want to be delivering a high level of skilled care that proves the patient couldn't have gotten better on their own. If you are continuing to prescribe visits and sessions for a patient to get them better, then your answer better be a resounding "Yes, they will decline without PT, and there is no way they can get this product at home!"

In many cases, asking this question will challenge therapists to question whether or not they are giving great technical care.

Traditional Clinic Service-Clinician Focus

Customer service is the core ingredient that differentiates a traditional clinic environment from a "Feel-Good Experience" environment. Historically, clinical healthcare service revolves *entirely* around the treating clinician. These environments are much like a team with one All-Star. Teams with one central All-Star rarely win championships, because there is only one person who can truly affect the outcome of the group. The other personnel orbit the professional, waiting on their every command, thus at the mercy of that individual's performance for the day.

Traditional clinic atmospheres tend to aggrandize the doctors or therapists in the office and minimize the contributions of the support staff. Team performance is based solely on one individual's talent and strengths. In these environments, the doctor's or physical therapist's attitude, skill, and temperament *is* the team. If the "All-Star" has an off day or becomes ill, the entire team suffers—and potentially loses clients.

The doctor or therapist who is the spotlighted All-Star rarely has the time or mental bandwidth to be present and aware of anything beyond the core physical diagnosis of the patient they are attempting to help. Although these All-Star clinicians are sought after for their healthcare skills, they tend to lack the relational skills, leadership skills, or teambuilding skills that enable the entire team to be involved in the care and recovery of the patients. "XYZ credentials and all the alphabet soup" behind a clinician's name might make them seem like the most important person in the room, but these titles create little to no value when it comes to getting patient results.

Let's take a side-by-side comparison of two PTs. One is simply a PT and the other is a PT, OCS, ATC. The higher education and credentials of being an orthopedic certified specialty and a certified athletic trainer do not guarantee higher skill, nor do the higher education and credentials guarantee they know how to create a great customer experience.

However, if the PT without any other credentials implements The Feel-Good Experience, by listening, and seeking to anticipate the patient's needs, they'll have a patient who has felt a connection and a great experience that they will attend all of their appointments, recover fully, and become a customer for life who would refuse to go to any other office. This is not to suggest a physical therapist with advanced education and training won't deliver great customer service and The Feel-Good Experience. I am merely establishing the fact that there is no correlation between more technical knowledge and greater customer service and satisfaction.

The training I received in physical therapy several decades ago revolved around a treatment-mindset. It was focused solely on evidence-based care, or the *X*s and *O*s of treatment. Simply put, if no scientific studies certify the treatment, there should be no treatment delivered.

Palliative measures—comforting the patient, being friendly, easing their pain, and truly "caring" for the patient as an individual—were seemingly viewed as lacking professionalism as they weren't considered part of a scientific method of "proper" physical therapy care. The nineties were a great time of expansion for the physical therapy profession as access started growing and more treatment options became available, but we had moved from high touch to high tech, removing some of the base personal attributes that made PTs unique to MDs. More connection, relationship, and psychology had been replaced with more technique, research, and evidence. I felt there had to be a place for both.

I recall specific lectures implying to avoid "relating," "sympathy," and any personal connection across professional boundaries. The traditional perception of healthcare service is, "I am the professional, and you are the patient. Don't cross that line." Strict role delineation between professional and patient bars any connection or warmth between the two individuals. That leaves the typical institutional, sterile, and cold feeling you get when you go into a clinic and you must speak to the receptionist behind a plexiglass sliding window.

When was the last time you received warm customer service where the person greeting you was behind a glass partition? My last experiences were in two places: a lone store merchant behind a bulletproof glass partition in a small, late-night convenience store, and a receptionist in a medical office. Neither had good customer service. Most *banks* have even removed the partitions to create a more open, warm, and friendly environment for patrons.

The glass partition does not convey messages of warmth, connection, friendliness, hospitality, or a desire to relate to the consumer. It implies the same message that a toll booth or a prison entry does: protection, distance, transaction, and segregation (of course, safety measures for COVID-19 have temporarily made this necessary, but the metaphor remains the same).

Creating boundaries and obstacles in a customer service environment diminishes any potential relationship and connection to a patient. Traditional attitudes, a focus on credentials, poor communication, a lack of empathy, and glass partitions are just a few of the issues existing in clinics that can create barriers. Barriers reduce trust, communication, and understanding of needs and wants.

The Physics of Customer Service: Speed, Energy, Motion, and Emotion

Serving as many customers as possible, as fast and as efficiently as possible, and with the highest quality possible is the key to success in customer service and, ultimately, business. **Speed and Energy**—keeping customers happy and moving swiftly in and out of the clinic with no wasted time—is a core principle in The Feel-Good Experience.

We want to give them what they want without hesitation. People who struggle to think quickly, are slow in speaking, or are slow to get things done tend to struggle in a highly successful, fast-paced, business-oriented environment. TFGE is designed to take all the small, problem-solving moments and automate them for action so movement continues without hesitation.

Optimal movement is "Goldilocks." To create the correct **energy and emotion** for an amazing experience, it can't be too fast or chaotic, and it can't be at a snail's pace, either. It's gotta be "just right." An optimal movement pace will feel just right to the patient. It will make them feel comfortable and in control, yet also like they are being led professionally. This perfect balance accentuates the positives any customer would seek during their physical therapy encounter. Positive energy is the catalyst for positive emotions.

Just like energy, **motion** is also a catalyst for positive **emotions** and mental aptitude. When you awake from sleeping, you haven't *moved* for hours and you are sluggish, slow, and your processing speed is dulled. Ultimately, everything is numb, suppressed, dormant, and could be categorized as "low motion and low emotion." Contrast that with your daily routine. You went to work. You moved and thought all day long. You picked kids up from school (*moving*), went to the gym (*moving some more*), and got groceries (*more moving and thinking*) before going home for the night. Now that you are home, you put your groceries away (*more moving*) and decide what to make for supper while helping your kids with homework (*a lot more moving and a lot more thinking*). Once all chores are done (*more moving*) and you settle in for evening, are you able to go straight to bed, or do you need some time to wind down from your "energy?"

This can be applied to our clinics. Movement starts to perpetuate more business and more patients will be willing to come in for care! Patients who come to our facilities for care all say that our environment is busy, yet very energetic and fun. The movement of our staff and our systems keeps the patient efficiently moving through our customer service stations (more on those later). Reducing the time they feel they are in our clinics keeps us respectful of their time.

Consider a chemistry example. Molecules start moving faster, expanding, and gaining energy once increased temperature is applied. Once a pot of simmering water generates its first bubble, in a very short time, there is a second bubble, then a third, and then it just exponentially starts bubbling over. That is the law of thermodynamics:[2] adding energy into a system to create action, movement, and intention.

Sir Isaac Newton said, "An object in motion stays in motion. An object at rest stays at rest."[3]

Our motion creates our emotion, and our emotion creates our motion. It has been shown in psychological research studies that if a depressed person simply focuses their mind on visualizing positive, active, energetic images, their heart rate increases and they actually begin increasing neurotransmitter activity such as dopamine and serotonin release. Their mind activity is enough of a perception to create actual physical movement within the cells of their body. *Emotion creates motion.*

One of the hallmark clinical treatments for patients with mood disorders such as depression, anxiety, chronic fatigue syndrome, and fibromyalgia is physical exercise.[4]

Exercise releases endorphins into our bloodstream and creates a pleasant feeling, so it elevates our mood and is shown to reduce the perception of "pain." *Motion creates emotion.* Our patients are active with exercise, and that alone can help generate improved feelings, but there are physical therapy clinics all across the country that work on exercises with patients in a quiet, sterile, serious environment under the guise of being a "professional" organization. Unfortunately, that experience is quite "vanilla" to the common consumer—and very technical. The perception is they got physical therapy, and that was it. If we're striving for excellence, we need to expect more from our clinics. Simply providing physical therapy services is not enough. We need to combine the motion of the physical exercise with the emotion of a positive environment to give our patients the most benefit.

Let's use leadership as an example. One single person can influence an entire movement of millions of people. How does one person shift a global mindset, start a revolution, or inspire humanitarian effort amongst total strangers? It occurs by one person deciding to "create movement" by *acting* upon deeply held, primal needs and desires that all humans innately have. Normal, healthy people all want to make positive, constructive actions, and they make their positivity spread by *emotionally* influencing someone else to copy them and behave the same way. This is exactly how modern pop culture marketing works to build a brand name that everyone wants to be a part of.

Each person on a team should be leading by creating movement, physically and emotionally, either with another staff member or a patient. We train in our clinics, constantly on the concept of leadership—leading ourselves first, and then leading others. Staff are also taught in TFGE to "pay it forward." Simply put, make the day of the person closest to you. Lighten their spirit and improve their physical speed by setting the pace of physical movement and stretching their limits of positive emotional influence. That person, now with lifted spirits and faster speed, is logically vibrating at a higher energy level or emotional state. That individual will come in contact with other staff and patients in the clinic, and their further interactions will create an exponential growth of positive emotions that can be felt palpably.

Joy attracts joy. Misery loves company.

TFGE Difference

Warm, accepting personalities create opportunities for communication and affinity between individuals.

Affinity, our likeability, is what enables a patient to be willing to share space, time, and money with us in our clinics. You create the warmth, connection, and relationship to attract and build them as a customer for life, and the business reaps the financial rewards of delivering a great service repeatedly. That is the win-win scenario of The Feel-Good Experience. A win for the customer means getting phenomenal care and being treated well, and a win for your business means growing and prospering.

Human beings are sociable in general, and people who go into healthcare certainly should care about people. It is impossible to care, connect, and help people if you refuse to share the same space with them.

The most basic component of a successful medical office visit consists of two people facing each other, openly communicating with no restrictions or barriers. That is the only way a true understanding of a patient's condition or feelings can occur. When barriers and obstacles are added into the equation, more complexity and greater limitations occur. Those barriers create a situation where a patient could, in theory, receive basic transactional healthcare, but they wouldn't receive a value-added experience that they would rave about. Remove the barriers!

Transactional Service vs. Experiential Service

The traditional model forces a culture of diminishing a person to their diagnosis. The doctor treats the back pain, skipping the fact that they are treating a *person* with back pain. This is important because one day that patient will (hopefully) not have back pain, and will remember how they were treated and what kind of experience they had at your facility.

If you want to deliver customer service, you have to reach the true, inner person, because the true person inside—the emotions, the feelings, the values, and the personality—is the driver that will decide whether or not they want to seek service from you again. You create or destroy the customer relationship by how you engage the "inner person" of each customer.

In the traditional clinic model, an equal exchange occurs because the doctor never discovers the inner person of each customer. Although this interaction is fair and equal, it tends to fall very short of five-star customer service as it lacks the extra "wow factor" and rush of emotions that an extra special experience can provide. Thus, the longevity of the customer relationship in the traditional clinic model is average to poor.

Instead of a growing, prosperous clinic that helps a lot of patients very effectively, these clinics work ten times harder than necessary, planting the burden entirely on one practitioner. Those clinics are overworked and tend to have staff discontent and poorer working conditions. Furthermore, those clinics—because they don't tend to see as many patients—don't earn the revenue that more successful practices do.

Cash flow shortage and a mentality of hyper-conservativism tend to create an environment that doesn't provide patients with simple necessities, such as updated equipment, a fresh coat of paint, new carpeting, or even simple cleanliness, simply because they have not learned how to cycle patients through systematically **without** making patients feel like they are being cycled through systematically!

Customer loss due to attrition is very costly to a business. It is six to seven times more expensive (and difficult) to attract a new patient who doesn't know you than it is to attract a patient who already knows, likes, and trusts you.[5]

Experiential models, such as The Feel-Good Experience, are superior at customer retention. Former patients are like family and friends, and that relationship is what keeps patients very satisfied. The loyal, raving fans keep businesses prospering.

We have many patients who come from across the state—three hundred miles or further—for our services. Some patients are willing to drive fifty to sixty miles for daily sessions with us because The Feel-Good Experience is relational and experiential, not transactional.

Prima Donna Practitioner vs. Altruistic Practitioner

Traditional clinic cultures can fall victim to prima donna practitioners who think they are better than the person they are relating to, thus they don't fully listen or stay present with the patient in the moment. Empathy is lacking, and that is a critical emotional skill in relationship building and customer service.

Medical providers having "god complexes" is nothing new, but when a therapist's inflated self-esteem goes unchecked, they can drive away customers that could have easily been retained. Those clients fleeing your practice will share their bad experience with twenty people working very hard against your practice reputation. In contrary, happy and satisfied clients will share their positive experience with only three.[6]

Plenty of forces are working against your practice and few are supporting it. Fortunately, all that is necessary to solve this problem is for therapists to be aware of patients' emotions, needs, and wants.

The other end of the continuum is the ultra-altruistic therapist who, in their very sensitive nature, doesn't consider anything else beyond the customer. This is the "bleeding-heart" therapist who takes the adage, "the customer is always right," to the extreme. This overzealous passion can lead to negative outcomes when the patient has poor intentions, poor compliance, or personal financial issues.

The zealots toward either end of the spectrum *can* succeed in these environments, if there is enough diversity of personalities alongside them in the practice. A variety of values and temperaments helps to balance the stronger extremes, thus stabilizing the natural order of the clinic environment and creating a win-win experience for the patient and the practice.

The key is in finding a balance, and TFGE helps you do that. You will naturally relate to the person, instead of thinking you're better than them or they're better than you. When you become more aware of this harmony, you will ensure a greater outcome for not only the patient, but the practice as well.

Team Quality vs. Individual Quality

Under the system of The Feel-Good Experience, we demand to always deliver high-quality service. We have a servant leadership model that reduces the importance, or dependency, of any one individual person on the team, including the practitioner. It takes that collective talent, strength, and skill and puts it all together into one system for the betterment of the team.

TFGE is energetic and efficient. It combines the talents of all supporting staff. We seek to recruit high-energy people with high self-esteem. We also look for those who are benevolent and team-oriented who can get results in their life. We aim to blend a thought-provoking, introspective therapist with someone on their immediate team who is charismatic, fun, and an incredible salesperson. Balancing one person's weaknesses with another person's strengths is how you build a great team.

We never build clinics or the company around individuals. Instead, our model focuses on building upon teams and principled systems of operation. Because of that core value, our practices are not disabled when staff members resign. We certainly miss them, and we feel their absence, but by the next day, it must be "business as usual." The same principled customer service skills are followed, just with different people operating as placeholders. Thus, it is even more critical that our model ensures a patient has a relationship with the practice, not a single staff member. When a patient has a relationship with only one staff member, it renders your team at risk, if or when that staff member resigns, as they have a high likelihood of taking that patient out of your practice with them as they leave.

Furthermore, if a team is following the TFGE principles, every patient should never be isolated and should have connections with at least three staff on the clinic team. Three layers of relationship is enough to establish a relationship and, ultimately, loyalty to the organization and not to any individuals. Chances are if a patient has three relationships with the team, employee engagement and customer service is high.[7]

Team relationship with patients not only provides a greater experience but also provides insurance to the team. Softening peaks and valleys is vital to business survival, particularly when you lose a talented valuable teammate that was popular with patients. And since staff will come and go in the business world, it is necessary to reduce the impact felt by their departure.

We strive for continuity of care and service that looks and feels the same to every customer, no matter who delivered the care and service. An automated team approach to service removes the burden on one "rainmaker" and spreads the load to *many* players.

This adds value to the customer experience and creates a scalable and efficient clinical model for business success.

We believe wholeheartedly that the system supersedes the individuals—or in other words, "Team over self."

Quantity vs. Quality Myth: Finding the Sweet Spot

Conventional logic with most PTs is simple: patient care quality suffers with increasing quantity of patients. Simply put, the busier you become, the worse your outcomes. This belief is pervasive and held as a strong core belief with many PTs; however, it is a destructive, self-limiting belief.

This "group think" value has originated from the belief that all healthcare has to be delivered "one-on-one." The rigidly held belief that the only person who can impact the patients' results, their condition, and their healing is the clinician or technician grows directly from the traditional, practitioner-focused culture discussed previously.

Therapists like structure and order and generally "color within the lines." Proof of that was discovered by various personality profiles performed in our company between 2006 and 2017. A variety of tests including DISC,[8] MBTI,[9] Jung Personality,[10] Real Colors,[11] Clifton Strengths Finders,[12] Values and Attributes Index,[13] et al, displayed a common theme that many clinicians prefer conservative, cautious, task-oriented, and process-dominated environments. Furthermore, therapists preferred these environments over people, relational, improvisational, or creative environments.

This is not to be misinterpreted that, clinicians do not like people or lack social skills. However, it does mean that their strengths and skills make them better at tasks and procedures over people and creativity. Furthermore, I see a great alignment with therapist's skills with being good doers, technicians, and scientists but not great salespeople, relationship builders or leaders and developers. This dominant personality directive renders our profession to succumb to an imbalanced, simplistic, one-dimensional, fixed models of patient care delivery. Most PTs I know prefer to work by themselves, in isolation. They want their own patients, their own schedule, and they don't want to see someone else's patients. They don't even like to share staff or equipment. They demand continuity and generally struggle with improvising and change. Service quality and clinic reputation eventually suffer in a slower, cautious, perfectionistic, high-maintenance environment because a team with this mindset cannot meet rising customer expectations and demands.

The American consumer becomes more and more demanding each year. They expect multiple product and service options to handle a variety of dilemmas and they want it to be provided instantly at or above where it was last year, for the same or lower cost than last year. That is not unreasonable...that is "the customer!"

A therapist who decides to work alone can only see the number of patients within their own personal limits of what they can manage, so they will never be able to expand. They have capped their own potential for how many patients they could see on their caseload. Placed against the rising cost of business, and the drastic reduction of health care insurance reimbursement, this scenario looks very bleak for a therapist with a silo mentality.

As previously stated, a team-oriented culture is far more superior at delivering fast service, great results, and cost-effective care. Time is money, therefore, the faster you can get patients seen effectively, with an amazing experience, the better. That is the customer service hospitality model for healthcare you need to choose.

Looking at the therapist in the previous example, if that same therapist adds a PTA or a PT Tech to their team, they can expand and see many more patients, more efficiently, all while maintaining high-quality standards. They have traded in the "quality only" mindset for an "optimizing" mindset that equals high quantity and high quality combined. Economies of scale determine that the investment in two practitioners seeing more patients would be more cost effective than one therapist seeing only their own patients based on capacities.[14] Considering the rapidly declining reimbursement rates for physical therapy over the past fifteen to twenty years, expansion not only improves customer service efficiency but also makes very good business sense.[15]

The value-added model of The Feel-Good Experience easily replaces a non-progressive, non-futuristic model that myopically focuses on the transaction of technical, evidenced-based healthcare. One that negates the importance of balancing quality outcomes, quality experiences, and patient satisfaction with logistics will face the economic realities of a declining clinic.

Our system enables multitasking to occur with minimal patient situations (i.e., mistakes or errors that upset the patient). It does that by having multiple sets of people involved in servicing the patient; this team-based, systematic approach grows each teammate's capabilities to handle more responsibilities. By removing the stagnant one-on-one model, where we can only focus on one single issue or task or person at a time, we can cover more potential issues, tasks, or people by covering zones. This ensures the patients are being served and always led. By having multiple sets of eyes from many different stations within the clinic, we can observe the clients' responses and react to them appropriately and constantly. For example, the standard medical receptionist who answers the phone and schedules appointments is currently laser-focused on those basic, robotic tasks. Those are "task-opportunity" environments. But within TFGE, we challenge our receptionists to have their "head on a swivel." They are trained to anticipate and be on the lookout for service opportunities, whether it be on phone calls, emails, walk-ins, offering coffee to those waiting, holding the door to someone coming in, or walking someone to their car.

This model gains more information about a client; keeps our staff stimulated, active, and engaged; and puts our team in a much better position to protect against any miscues, misunderstandings, or negative patient situations.

The Need for a System

TFGE is a system. Systems are designed to eliminate the need to reinvent the wheel. By building around automated, subconscious actions that are necessary for flow and process, we save our energy and mental bandwidth for more pressing, detail-focused issues, such as the actual patient treatment progression and the patients' nonverbal cues and responses.

Mental energy vanishes quickly when time is spent in deep thought and processing. Unfortunately, in chaotic, disorganized, or emotionally toxic environments, most of a person's energy can be expended on unnecessary tasks and issues.

Burning energy on trying to find where you left your keys or your phone is hardly a critical or appropriate use of your mental or emotional capacity when you have a patient coming in with a lot of pain who is also very disengaged due to their recent divorce. You need your "A-Game" of vital energy and complete focus to deliver an experience and an emotional connection to this person that will impress them. If you lack an energy reserve, you won't pick up on cues and be able to shift from physical therapist to more of a counseling therapist, which is what that patient might need that particular day from their PT session. You must be aware, sensitive, and always intuitive to what mood the patient is in.

Time spent in a cycle of think, start, stop, and think again is an absolute waste when most of your actions are repeatable. A system will help you adopt step-by-step processes to service more patients with much less mental effort.

Clinics and teams that work in these siloed models with no human automation or systematic "recipe" to their processes create waste by inefficiency. Their lack of expansion due to inefficiency is extremely costly and cuts into each clinic's revenue—revenue that could have been used for business expansion, equipment, raises, or benefits.

Let's take an example. Two patients arrive at a clinic at the same time. One patient had an appointment; the other patient had a personal scheduling conflict, but had time now, so was checking availability. The patient with the scheduling conflict states their situation very clearly: "If they can't be treated now, they will cancel and not return."

The action taken by most clinics would be to cancel this walk-in patient, as reception and therapists would focus on the "burden" and would be unable to clearly see any possibility the patient could be treated. In the end, due to their lack of innovation, assertiveness, and grit, the therapist and the practice would lose a session and probably the patient entirely. The fact that the patient said, "they will cancel and not return" is enough of a threat to retaining this customer for life.

This patient is, obviously, very busy and doesn't have time to adjust their schedule due to other engagements. They are expressing to the staff that they demand some flexibility from others in their life. It's highly possible that they demand flexibility from all businesses that they patronize. This patient is also communicating that their needs and wants are for them to have greater control in setting their schedule.

Patients like this tend to create disturbances and frustrations with most PT clinics. I have witnessed staff reacting to this patient by internalizing their frustration or simply being super structured "according to policy" and refusing to negotiate with the patient. The scary part is, most therapists, receptionists, and even clinic owners don't realize there is a very clear and present danger of losing this patient to your competition.

These clients are no-nonsense and demand service when they want it according to their schedule, which means they are probably a very driven Type-A level personality. This type of personality tends to be very direct so could create some bad PR for your clinic reputation if they can't get care for their back pain as they intended. So, is it worth it to seek perfection in each patient's time slot of care on the schedule, or would it be a better decision to fit them in and surround them with a team that starts the process with a menu-style treatment, where whoever is available on the team takes care of them? Studying twenty years' worth of patient session data from typical outpatient PT practices reveals that nearly 80 percent of all sessions or higher follow the exact same cycle of "warm up, activity, cool down," like a gym fitness regimen. So eight out of ten times, a therapist will set a plan of care resembling this three-step pattern, so no need to have a patient sit idly in the waiting room. Get Them Started!

Both patients come out of this scenario satisfied, and the practice salvaged an appointment from being cancelled. That is simply good service, good business, and truly a win-win outcome. These situations arise without warning and can only be resolved optimally, if the staff or team is willing to be creative, seek opportunities and solutions, and be willing to make things work out for everyone involved.

In an experiential service practice, such as we are, a therapist has a schedule full of appointments, like other clinics. However, our clinicians also have a team circling around them to assist when these kinds of scenarios occur. We call it "playing a zone vs. man to man," which will be covered in detail in chapter 3. An adjacent therapist would take on the client and would use the aides and other PTAs to augment their care so the patient could progress in their rehabilitation. Remember, it's not about the specific therapist or the techniques they're using. It's about the principles of "perception of care."

Finally, when the original therapist was freed up, they could pick their second patient back up and finish their session with them. Both patients would be totally treated appropriately and legally, with appropriate use of licensed and unlicensed personnel.

If every teammate involved followed the correct playbook, *TFGE: Skills 1 through 4,* the patient will not have any concerns and will have been treated incredibly well. In fact, they may decide that they like the other therapist better and wish to transfer care over to them. Either way, the patient got serviced and was pleased. The clinic was able to handle a potential bottleneck on the schedule that other PT clinics would have struggled with. Patients have come to like the "urgent care" model that we have, where walk-ins are received and treated within the hour.

What appeared to be a challenge for therapists working as individuals can now be easily solved by two teammates working together. Their selfless nature allowed fast and effective patient treatment in order to optimize their overall team outcome. Once the focus becomes "what needs to be done" vs. "who is required to do it," the system flows smoothly.

Rewiring the PT Brain

There is a pervasive mindset with PTs that in order to deliver high-quality patient care, they have to see fewer patients and have a schedule that is perfectly controlled with no changes. Therapists, by nature, are "C&S" personalities, according to the DISC personality profile;[16] thus, they are very cautious, conservative, and scientific.

They also have great analytical skills, which is important for working with patients and making the correct decisions. Unfortunately, therapists also tend to lack confidence and certainty. This lack of self-assuredness leaves them wondering whether the hoofprints they heard could in fact be made by a zebra and not a horse. In other words, they second-guess the logical, more likely answer.

The desire to be perfect or exact dulls our creative thinking in favor of focusing on the what-ifs. Knowing that PTs in general have some of these self-limiting belief patterns, I wanted to help PTs retrain and challenge their belief systems about patient care. Furthermore, I wanted to improve PTs' outcomes and satisfaction by challenging them to adapt to a model that more closely resembles retail business models. Assimilation to a general public business environment will protect them and their careers. Insurance reimbursements are shrinking rapidly, with some insurances dropping physical therapy coverage. To survive, a PT and their clinic have to be exceptional in customer service.

What Does the Customer Want?

One of my mantras has always been "The day I quit thinking like a therapist was the day I became a great therapist." This is the truth! I had plenty of training, certifications, and knowledge, but I listened to the powers of the physical therapy profession instead of listening to my patients. I kept becoming frustrated by my inability to get people better quickly, so I quit trying so hard and started simplifying my approach.

I started using the old medical adage: "Listen to your patients. They will tell you exactly what to do to treat them."[17]

Physical therapists, unfortunately, view the quality argument from their own perspective, not the patient's viewpoint. There is not a physical therapist alive who believes they give poor quality care. Most will say they use "evidence-based paradigms" in all of their treatment plans. My response to anyone in PT who feels that quality care means using outcome studies and evidence-based practice (EBP) is, "Try promoting that to the general public and see how many new patients you get."

The general consumer who has low back pain is not thinking about which professional is using theoretical treatment models. They expect you to be a licensed professional who knows what they are doing. All they want is for you to get rid of their pain and get them back to normal. The rest of the shop talk and -isms that PTs place so much value in is stuff that nobody else knows or cares about.

Instead of using complex techniques or long, arduous, and strange rehabilitative sessions, I kept all my sessions simple, approximately one hour or so, and I *always* use some pain-relieving treatments that make patients feel good and that they actually wanted, such as massage, heat, ultrasound, infrared, laser and muscle stimulation.

Those subtle, small adjustments to my approach enabled me to gain the trust and acceptance of my patients. I was able to improve my patients' perception of my care and service, and then they consistently returned for their follow-up appointments. I started getting people better, and it became a much easier workload.

Patients with pain got treated with compassion and concern, were given some relief in our sessions, and then chose to return. In order to be a great PT, you must stop thinking like a PT.

Patient or Customer?

People receive the reverential title of "patient" in the medical world, but they are, in simple terms, a customer, and like any other customer, they want a product that will handle some sort of problem, want, or need in their life. They want that product to be *effective, efficient, and economical.* The patient/customer is just like you. You also want to buy products and services that are useful, provided without hassle, and are at an affordable price point.

More Customers = More Energy

In the TFGE Difference section, we discussed how quantity does not reduce quality. Therapists and other medical experts fall into a culture of "less equals better" or "less equals higher quality." They believe if they have too many patients, they will give worse care to each of them, and the patients will *feel* like they'll get less care. We need to change that mindset.

My counterargument to those in that mindset is, do you prefer to go to a restaurant, hotel, concert, or venue that is totally vacant of people? Doesn't it speak volumes about the attraction and popularity of a sports team, a musician, a restaurant, a hotel, or any venue, if they are busy and have a full parking lot?

The truth about any empty venue is that it is lifeless. Empty restaurants, vacant hotels, abandoned sidewalks in business districts, vacant city parks, empty golf courses, empty baseball stadiums, barren swimming pools—all these environmental images shout, "Something is wrong!" There is no life, spirit, or energy because there are no people.

Full parking lots, busy restaurants, roaring sports stadiums, or packed theatres with the sounds of its patrons' screams or belly laughs send a strong emotional message about the *value* those entities provide the consumer. On a subconscious level, we *all* feel better when we are walking into a full, vibrant, bursting venue. Our subconscious desire for conformity and validation to follow the herd is satisfied when we see that "everyone else" is also going to the same place we are.

I have worked in and analyzed customer service-related environments for over thirty years. I worked in the newspaper business, the grocery store business, the bar tending business, and the physical therapy business. I have been the customer, the server, and the supervisor of the servers. I have concluded that fewer consumers in a given clinic at a specific time does *not* add any value to the consumer whatsoever. The belief that "fewer patients equals greater quality care" is not scientifically valid.

Thomas McCafferty said, "The market is always right,"[18] no matter how conflicted our feelings can be as a society. Success is success! If a stock rises, business grows, profits soar, and customers flock in droves, it is *all* because of the demand that has been created due to human nature; needs and wants.

If there were no "created demand," there would be no patients, clients, or paying customers. The stock would decline, businesses would close, and unemployment would skyrocket. Fewer phone calls, fewer promotional ads, fewer staff, and fewer customers all equal less force, less inertia, less momentum, less movement, and less energy, which translates into fewer customers served, less revenue received, and fewer profits accumulated.

By increasing the number of people in the clinic, you will add **movement**. That movement adds **energy**! More patients and more staff moving quickly to service every client should create a clinic buzzing with atmosphere. As mentioned in the core concepts, motion and emotion are interchangeable. One begets the other, positively or negatively. Remember that guy Newton?

The Delta: Leading Change for the Better

While if you implement TFGE you will see change, this is not a quick-fix. TFGE is the long game, not the short game, so do not get frustrated and give up if it doesn't work immediately. Leading change is much like walking up a flight of steps. You have to go from step one to step two, never from step one to step twenty. It's a process that takes leadership, awareness, intuition in reading people, and recognition of when you are moving at the correct pace.

Leading physical or emotional movement must occur gradually. Since you don't expect an instant transformation in your patients, it isn't fair to expect that from your employees and your clinic. Transferring physically from constant wheelchair sitting to standing for two minutes straight is a considerable physical change. It takes many small steps to achieve that feat. In the same vein, we would never consider moving someone from a state of apathy and depression to a state of happy dancing.

A more appropriate gradient move might be to get someone who is solemn to simply open up and talk. That adjustment alone would be an enormous win for both the patient and the company.

Giving Quality Care

So we can see that TFGE is all about giving holistic quality care and extending beyond relieving the patient (customer's) pain. Somewhere, in every doctor's office or PT clinic brochure, there is a statement about how they deliver "the highest quality of care." However, too often, "quality" is only defined by medical standards, not by patient standards—and certainly not by any customer service standards. The Feel-Good Experience emphasizes determining "quality care" as defined by patients' perceived care and satisfaction.

So how does one do that? Well, that is the point of this book. But before we dive into the specifics, let's get an overarching view of how you achieve this.

The Customer: A Lot to Learn in Little Time!

Obviously, we can't know every single person and have a baseline of their emotions and personalities before they start in physical therapy. We can only evaluate them at face value as they present to us. Over time, session after session, you should be able to sense, analyze, and predict their behaviors, likes, dislikes, and values. By paying attention, you can go deeper with the person so you can learn enough about them to lead them accordingly.

People are like icebergs. Only a very small part of us, our outward behaviors, is visible above the surface. Most of our composition, the real us, and who we are, is deep beneath the surface. Yet it's that deep, real us that creates the behaviors on the outside. Eventually, who we truly are, rises to the surface, no matter how deep and invisible it appears.

Using the Hemingway Iceberg Theory of Behavior, illustrated below,[19] "We tend to only deal with what we perceive with the naked eye and the rest goes unnoticed." However, if we use this theory proactively, we can service patients beyond their expectations, because we are willing to not simply act upon what's obvious but to find out what is beneath.

In order to get below the surface, to the "real" them, you must learn their thoughts. Now, unless you are a mind-reader, you will have to ask some questions, gather their opinions, and link their behavior to their mindset (thoughts). Once you can get a person talking about their thoughts and you learn their beliefs and their feelings (emotions), then they will express their true, deep intrinsic needs. You won't be perfect at it; after all, people can be extremely complex, but this strategy gets you as close as possible.

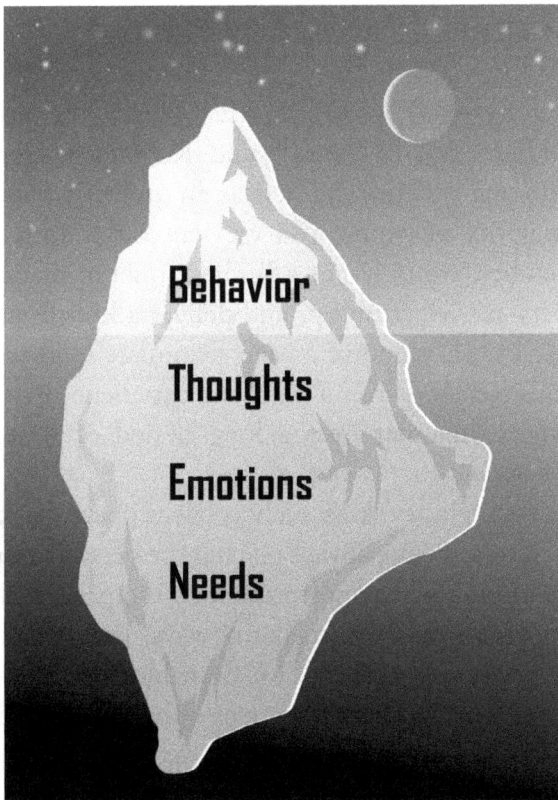

Married couples who have spent upward of sixty years together have commented that they still are getting to know and understand this person with whom they are so intimately familiar. In business encounters, we have far less time. An hour of physical therapy three days per week is not nearly enough time to learn everything about a patient in order to perfectly serve them. We have to use a broad, overarching system to cover all of the major possibilities of engagement to deliver the best customer service experience possible.

Umbrella Policy for Customer Service

TFGE is a four-skill paradigm that blends the principles of Maslow's Hierarchy of Needs[20] and Robbins 6 Core Human Needs[21] into one system. This acts as an umbrella policy to cover the vast majority of people you will encounter in a very quick way. Remember, we only get a limited amount of time to evaluate the person, size them up, and deliver a knock-out, five-star experience. TFGE empowers each teammate (and team) collectively to consistently deliver a high-end experience in a repeatable and sustainable manner over a long period of time, ensuring long-term success.

This success includes skills such as friendliness, basic technical discussion of treatments, always placing the person in a position of strength, and building empowerment so the patient always feels free to express themselves. In many ways, the ultra-simple and casual conversational style of TFGE enables subtle changes that we sometimes can't perceive ourselves—that is, until the patient's spouse calls to tell us how much improved their loved one's physical and emotional behaviors have been since they began coming to physical therapy. Those testimonials are totally a reason to celebrate, as that is our end goal with TFGE!

Constructive positive energy started by one single person moves through another and, eventually, the entire team to affect literally everyone in the facility. This positive emotional state *is* what the core of healing, wellness, and living a life of fulfillment is about. There are numerous accounts of people overcoming cancer when the odds were scientifically not in their favor. The patient's sheer will to fight and survive and their energy emitted has been reportedly felt by many a healthcare provider in oncology. All too often, we discredit a human being's spirit, beliefs, and emotions as a critical aspect of healing and recovery.

80/20 Model to Quality Care

The formula for improving your quality of care as a clinician is simple. Focus 20 percent of your energy on your technical abilities—meaning the tactical, automated tasks an experienced clinician can do in their sleep. Focus the remaining 80 percent of your energy on your customer service and perceived abilities, also known as soft skills. Citing Pareto's Principle of 80/20,[22] any therapist who is spending 80 percent of their time on their technical skills is focusing on the weak link of the quality care formula. This does *not* mean that a therapist should have poor clinical skills. Quite the contrary. They should always be advancing their diagnostic- and treatment-related skills. However, we believe that a *combination* of continuing education for treatment skills *and* skill development in communication, sales abilities, influence, listening, and people skills is vital to improving the customer experience.

The Product of Emotional Intelligence Management (EQ over IQ)

The Feel-Good Experience is all about how a patient feels regarding their encounter with you. So if they come in feeling indifferent, you will need to tap into the core emotional competency of inspiring performance so they are then led to the productive state of empowerment. Your goal is to take customers from an unproductive state to a productive one as illustrated by the table below.

A patient with positive, "feel good" emotions is in a better place, personally speaking, than someone without those emotions. The patient can feel these positive emotions during, after,

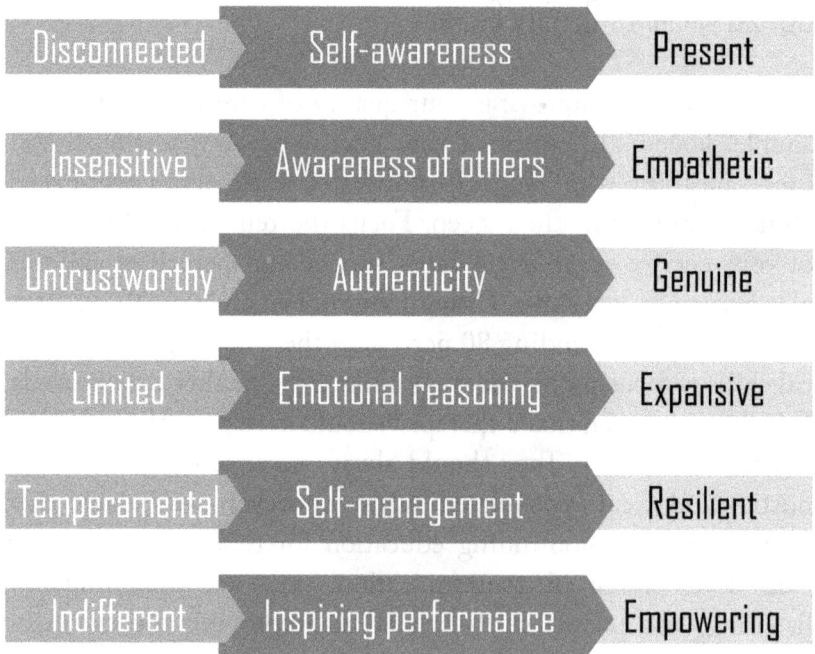

Disconnected	Self-awareness	Present
Insensitive	Awareness of others	Empathetic
Untrustworthy	Authenticity	Genuine
Limited	Emotional reasoning	Expansive
Temperamental	Self-management	Resilient
Indifferent	Inspiring performance	Empowering

Source: Inner Citadel Consulting www.innercitadelconsulting.com

and before their sessions. You should seek, at minimum, to have a patient "feel good" during their session. You can then stretch their Feel-Good Experience to have the positive emotions linger long after their session. Once you have done that, you are on your way toward mastering the delivery of The Feel-Good Experience. Your ultimate service delivery involves managing patients' emotions during, after, and before the next session or next time they see you. Simply put, always be shifting a patient's emotions to the positive at all times, in every encounter, in every conversation, and in every anticipated need or want that they have.

To do this, you must be skilled in emotional intelligence or "EQ." Daniel Goleman, who founded the term, used "EQ" in comparison to IQ.[23] Physical Therapists have a high IQ, but a high EQ is what will create a close personal connection, the intangibles that keep the patients coming back.

The chart on page 40 outlines the structure of EQ and shows what you need to be aware of to effectively lead and influence another person's emotions and attitudes. Notice how you must first have your own self-awareness?

Value-Added Healthcare

The Feel-Good Experience exists to provide an added-cost value to patients beyond their simple physical treatment.

Adding additional, "no-cost" service options into a patient's care creates a much more valuable service. PT competitiveness depends entirely on the concept of "positioning." You need to position PT values against the various other health options (e.g., chiropractic, massage therapists, pharmaceutical options) and show why PT is the best choice. Increasing value in PT sessions creates an increasing commitment to the completion of their plan

Self   Social

	Self	Social
Recognition	**Self-awareness** • Emotional-awareness • Accurate self-assessment • Self-confidence	**Social awareness** • Empathy • Organizational awareness • Service orientation
Regulation	**Self-management** • Self-control • Transparency • Adaptability • Achievement drive • Initiative	**Relationship management** • Inspirational leadership • Developing others • Influence • Change catalyst • Conflict management • Buiilding bonds • Teamwork and collaboration

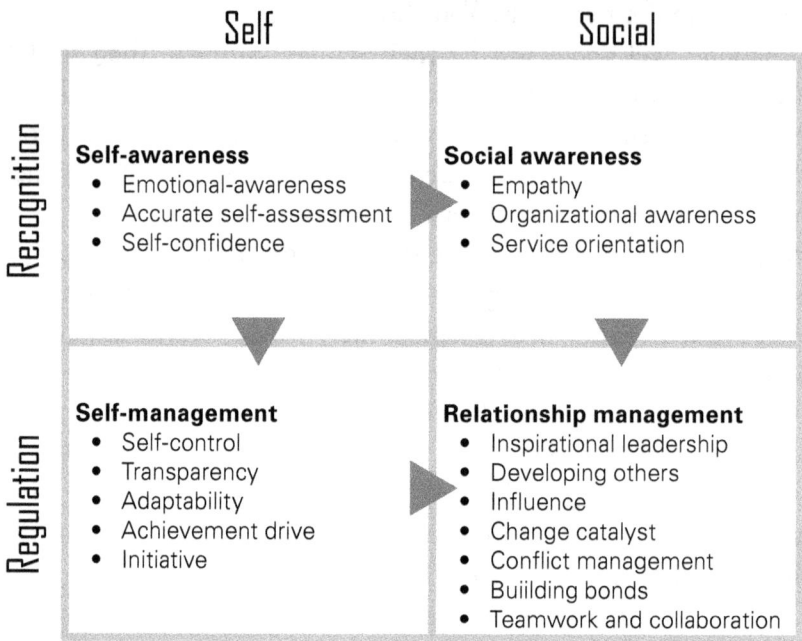

Components of Emotional Intelligence (EI/EQ)

of care and reduces the chances of a patient trying another option. Simply put, don't deliver physical therapy—deliver an experience!

TFGE System Intro

The core of The Feel-Good Experience is creating product quality via the emotional state of the patient. The number of positive emotions and the duration of those emotions determine the quality rating of The Feel-Good Experience.

The specific emotional triggers in use are as numerous as people's individualities, experiences, and personalities. They are infinite.

Studies have shown that all people have similar needs and wants. The Feel-Good Experience system targets all those general needs and wants into two categories: Structural and Relational. These categories are addressed within a layered, four-skill process.

In order to lead a patient's emotional states, you want to implement all four skills in The Feel-Good Experience.:

Skill 1: Create Positive Perception of Care

Skill 2: Create Positive Moments (through Clinic Stations & Zones)

Skill 3: Create a Win-Win Outcome

Skill 4: Create An Experience (not physical therapy)

TFGE is an easy system based upon simple skills and fundamentals. You must build the foundational skill on the pyramid before advancing to the next skill, or the pyramid will topple over.

The Feel-Good Experience can be installed brick by brick to grow with each patient. This system is designed to be used by staff individually but grows in scale for a team. There are also "safety nets" to catch breaks in service, as nobody is perfect in every skill. Therefore, skill priorities are crucial. You can't "cherry-pick" skills, because the other skills will lose their effectiveness rapidly. This system is simple, yet the details are many. It's important to start with the fundamental basics, and then to build upon that platform.

TFGE in a Nutshell

The Feel-Good Experience is emotional leadership and management. In other words, TFGE is attitude and decision management. Research has shown that optimistic people have greater health

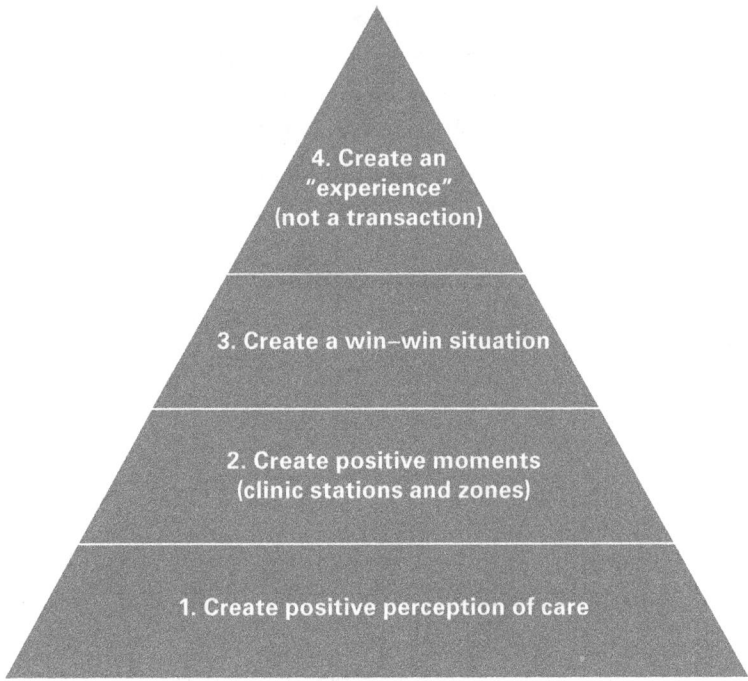

and success,[24] so it stands to reason that if you learn how to manage a patient's emotions positively, you will create in their minds a positive attitude about their experience with you, which will subsequently affect their decisions. Those decisions include their commitment to their sessions, making them customers for life. TFGE pays enormous dividends for you and your customers, both personally and professionally.

Chapter 2

Skill 1: Create
a Positive Perception of Care

Perceived Care Is Greater
than Technical Care Alone

If I told you that "perception of care" is more important than actual technical care, would you believe me?

How often have you gone to a restaurant with amazing food, yet they gave poor service, had slow waiters, miscalculated your bill, and confused your order? Even if the food were truly incredible and award winning, we'd still call that a bad experience and might hesitate to go back to that restaurant.

Contrast that experience to a restaurant that has fast, friendly service; amazing accuracy of your order; and prompt attention to every need and want. Now that's better. You leave this place happier and feel like you had a great experience overall. Your time was not wasted, and you'll probably go back. Do you really care that the food wasn't prepared by an award-winning chef? Nope! All you know is your perception of service was excellent! That is the core of The Feel-Good Experience: great *perceived* product quality.

Product quality is the foundation; therefore, it's the most important of all the skills. The skill of creating positive perceived care is the most valuable skill you can build when developing customer service excellence in *any* job.

Great product quality is measured by having good technical clinical care surrounded by great perceived care.

Complete product quality includes the actual physical core product or service as well as all the customer-related pathways and experiences to reach, access, receive, accept, and satisfactorily pay for said "product."

A couple of simple questions flush out the confusion that most in the business and service industry have. Did the product or service do what it was intended to do from the customer's viewpoint? How was the product or service packaged, offered, delivered, and charged? In ALL businesses, it's not just what we are buying, but how we are buying it.

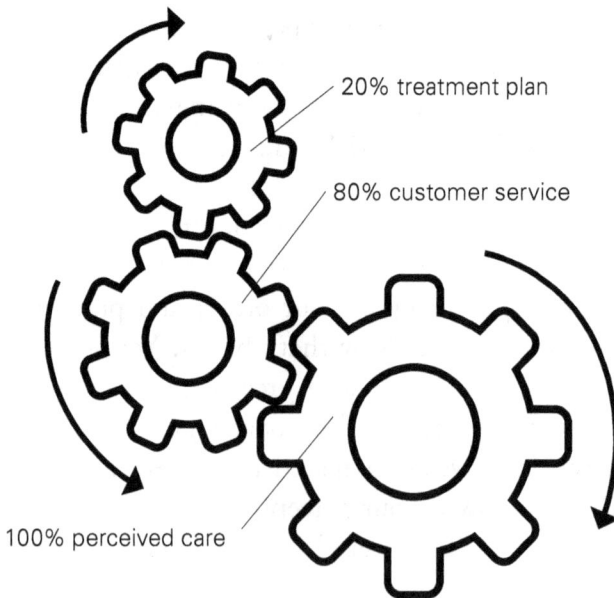

20% treatment plan

80% customer service

100% perceived care

So, what is perceived care? Merriam-Webster defines perceived as "becom[ing] aware of through sight, hearing, touch, taste, or smell."[25] In other words, we need to focus on positively influencing a person through their various senses. We engage with and make sense of the world around us with our five senses. TFGE uses the five senses to positively stimulate the most primal positive emotions.

To deliver great perceived care in the TFGE model, you need the team-based approach as discussed in chapter 1. In the team model, the entire team—including the clinicians—is charged with the responsibility of creating the Perceived Level of Care.

Perception of Care: The Parable of the Two Parties

Picture this: You have been invited to two parties. At the first party, you are met immediately at the door with a smile. Someone takes your coat and makes you feel very warm and welcome. They make you feel valuable, like their party would not be as fun without you there! They direct you to where the food and drinks are and make sure you are provided a place to sit if you wish. You are then introduced properly to other people at the party, as the host continues to ensure that you feel included, valuable, and ultimately, that you are having a great experience! Any early sign of exit, any observation of you sitting isolated in the corner with no one talking to you is addressed immediately by the host talking to you and starting up a new conversation.

All the way outside to your car, you are still laughing and talking about the party. You are still filled with positive feelings when you arrive at the second party. You go up to the door to ring the doorbell. You don't hear anything inside. It sounds very quiet, so you ring the doorbell again. Finally, the host answers the door and seems uninterested that you are there. You are not called by name, not greeted by even a smile. The host quickly gets called over to one of their friends and leaves you standing alone in a living room of people who are sitting and looking half asleep. They are certainly not sociable or inclusive at all.

After standing alone in the living room entryway for a while, not included in any conversations and not shown where food and drinks can be found, you are feeling generally miserable, uninvolved, not engaged, not cared about, neglected, and eventually rejected and out of place. You decide that you want to laugh and feel welcome again, so you head back over to the first party!

This metaphor describes the difference between a traditional clinic service model based entirely on mechanical, non-feeling processes (a house, a party, what else did you expect?), and a clinic that uses The Feel-Good Experience (greeted, led through the house, included, introduced, provided for, and sad to see you go upon exit).

Couldn't you tell how the party was going to be by your first impression? In other words, your perception of the party was determined by the first encounter you had. Perceived care starts immediately upon the consumer entering the building! Within the first minute, the consumer will make a judgment (right or wrong) about their perception of you, your team, and your service. Make that first impression count, and in all things, treat the consumer as a guest in your home.

And that first impression comes from using all five senses, as mentioned earlier, and communicating effectively.

Communication Awareness

Poor communication leads to many problems, disagreements, and misunderstandings, whereas good communication leads to understanding, awareness, agreement, rapport, and buy-in. Communication can be seen as a formula with verbal and non-verbal components. The **verbal** component is made up of literally the words we speak. The **nonverbal** component is made up of tone of voice and body language (including posture and facial expressions).

Nonverbal communication contains two of the three components of communication, but as you can see from the pie chart, it actually composes 93 percent of our entire communication! We can present ourselves positively or negatively without realizing it, due to not being aware of this formula. In order to direct others' interpretations or perceptions of us, we *need* to know how to manage our nonverbals. The good news is we can control this with self-awareness of our posture, our vocal tone, our facial expressions, and our arm and body positioning.

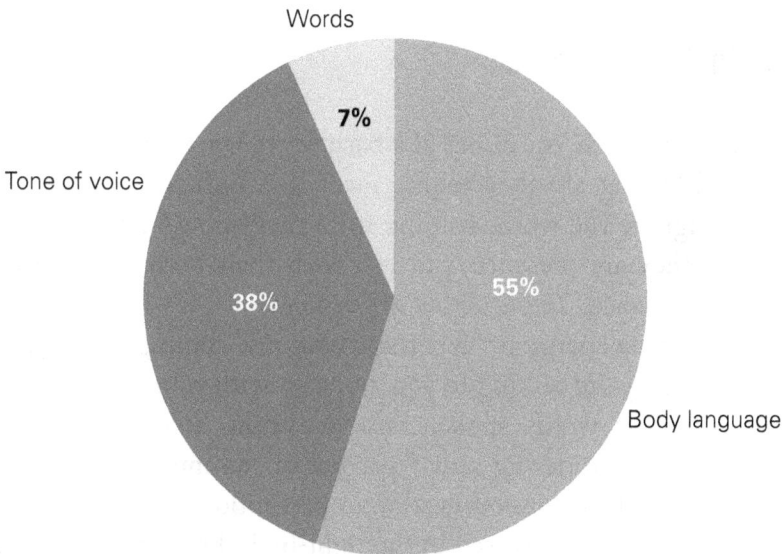

Words

7%

Tone of voice

38%

55%

Body language

What makes up what we "hear." Adapted from Albert Mehrabian. *Nonverbal Communication* (New Brunswick, NJ: Aldine Transaction, 2007).

Once you build this body awareness and vocal communication skills, you can then evaluate what nonverbal messages the consumers are sending to you. You can start perceiving *their* attitude and emotions toward you, toward your teammates, and toward the entire company. This is an invaluable tool in determining whether you and your team are creating a great perception of care.

Advancing these communication and emotional management skills will allow you to not only react to situations effectively but also give you command over the consumer's feelings. You will be able to lead consumers from a lower, negative, or unhappy state to a higher, satisfied state *before they were even aware of their own dissatisfaction.*

Becoming acutely aware of someone's nonverbals and taking an active genuine interest in them will determine how deep of a connection you can make with them, which in turn affects how likely they are to have a Feel-Good Experience.

How to Read Nonverbals

When reading the consumer at a basic level, you will want to ask yourself, "What are they telling me?" It is difficult, at first, for most to ignore the words coming from their mouth and to listen to what they are presenting to you with their body, eyes, arms, and tone of voice. *This is the art of listening.*

It takes true energy to "feel the vibrations" coming from a person while they are talking to you, to listen with your meta-senses. Processing the words spoken is a left-brain, analytical/logical exercise, but considering only 7 percent of communication is the actual words, true communication or perception of one's communication has to be processed in the right-brain hemisphere, where subjectivity, feelings, emotions, and arts are all housed. Full, complete communication takes both the left and right brain—meaning is sensed, not analyzed.

In the end, words tell you what they want in a basic way, but what you should *really* care about is how the person feels about you and your team. The answer to that question will determine whether or not they will attend their next appointment, or if they will ever return in the future.

So, how do you read someone's nonverbals? To get better at reading their nonverbals so you know what they care about, spend more time studying a variety of people and behaviors. This will improve your intuition and improve your sense of how people show their emotions without using words. Crossing arms, avoiding eye contact, adopting a slumped posture, turning their body position away, pausing or lagging in responses, stuttering, twitching or an inability to be still, speaking too softly or too loudly, and interrupting are all generally indicators of defensive, negative, or repelling emotions. If you see these, they indicate a lack of connection. Keeping an eye out for signals like this is all part of the evaluation of human communication.

Let's take tone as an example. The vocal tone is likened to music: it's either a screeching out-of-tune song or a beautifully composed opera. Which is your voice?

Your facial expressions and your body posture can immediately create a positive or negative tone within your voice. Try smiling before saying the word "Hello." Then try saying "Hello" while frowning. Can you perceive the difference in the sound quality and invitation in your voice? Try saying "Hello" with different emotions. What does your voice sound like when scared, happy, angry? Facial expressions, thoughts, emotional states, and your overall demeanor determine the quality, authenticity, and professionalism of your vocal-tone quality. Saying happy words while giving off unhappy verbal cues is kind of like trying to sing a slow tender love song to the aggressive fast beats of an AC/DC tune. It's not in alignment and therefore *not* congruent or believable. This change happened merely because of a small, nonverbal facial-expression adjustment.

When you say you are very pleased to see someone, yet your vocal tone is inexpressive, monotone, and lifeless, and your body language is "arms crossed and not facing them," then your communication presentation is not inviting or believable. Once you align the words you are saying with your vocal-tone quality and body language, your communication becomes believable.

The consumer will believe and ultimately buy into your actions and your presentation over your words. According to the Pew Research Center in 2019, only 17 percent of the polled American public found elected politicians "trustworthy" due to their tendency to promise with words but deny follow through with action.[26] Be very aware of your nonverbals so you display exactly what you are saying.

By developing the skills of reading people effectively so you can best serve them, you are anticipating their needs before they tell you what they need. That is when you start to WOW customers!

Get to Know Your Patients

As you communicate and pick up on their nonverbals, you need to keep your biases in check. An objective, nonjudgmental attitude to oneself and others can enable us to assess the needs and wants of the consumer more accurately. By removing preconceived biases, we are better equipped to serve the customer, and we are better equipped to get to know our customers.

In order to truly know your customers or patients, you have to know who they are as people. You have to start with their basic needs and what they are there being treated for, of course, but to take it to the TFGE level, you will have to learn more about them. Talk about their likes, dislikes, work, family, hobbies, and interests, and you will show respect and honor to the other person in your interest in them.

Landmines and Pet Peeves

Customer Service is neither an exact science nor a perfectly correlative relationship of actions to outcomes. There are, however, a few general pet peeves of mine that you should avoid in order to make the consumer happy.

Poor Results on Day One

In physical therapy, if we make a patient's symptoms worse, we have to do some serious explaining and preparation to resolve their symptoms as soon as possible. Even making them sore can turn them off your care, so the first day has to be extremely gentle. Use an abundance of communication, discussion, education, and specific details, yet keep it as simple as possible to reduce confusion. The patient should know, in simple terms, exactly why they may be sore the next day, or why their conditions might worsen, and that we took responsibility for this.

Poor results upon the first encounter are pretty self-explanatory as a huge landmine in your success of TFGE. When the client's problem is not improved or is, in fact, worsened, they likely will quit and try another provider. Keep day one simple and do everything you can to ensure a positive encounter.

Waiting beyond Ten Minutes Is Unacceptable

Many consumers have become used to waiting for longer than ten minutes in bigger medical offices, but for a typical physical therapy office (considering there are many competitive options for treatment), anything that creates a detraction from a great experience should be avoided. Time is a precious commodity in all of our lives, so we cannot afford to waste it in any manner.

Long wait times can be avoided or at least lessened by communication and teamwork. Making your staff fully aware of the danger of long wait times can help reverse engineer how to ensure this doesn't happen. If you find yourself behind, you can catch up in two ways: work faster or prioritize actions. I have often witnessed teammates confuse "vital" actions with "non-vital" actions. This can result in a really busy environment with a full schedule and plenty of phone inquiries, yet with 10 to 20 percent of your staff—based on Pareto's Principle—reviewing the mail or cleaning the coffee pot. Those are important actions that *do* need to be done at some point within the workday, but during this busy bottleneck in the schedule, your employees have other things to prioritize—like answering the phones or greeting clients at the door. In other words, they need to work on the vital actions only. This ensures not one minute of opportunity will be wasted on the patient or the practice.

In a growing, prosperous business, your number one goal should be to service current clients and to reach for growth through new clients. In order to survive in business, it is never acceptable to be complacent with an environment that is "busy." Growth and expansion occur by stretching and improving systems' efficiencies, particularly in customer service.

Driving as a metaphor applies here. When on a rural country road with no traffic, you can relax, reduce your speed, and drive with less focus. However, the second you pull on to the interstate with heavy traffic at seventy to eighty miles per hour, your attention to all details and focus are paramount in order to stay safe and get to your destination. Focusing on the flow of customers and keeping things running on time is the best way to ensure minimal wait times. If that means that another therapist needs to take the patient who has been waiting longer than ten minutes, that is what needs to happen. The problem in delays, most of the time, isn't the patient but the speed and focus of the therapist. Speed, promptness, and accuracy are the hallmark drivers of great customer service and The Feel-Good Experience.

Sober, Inexpressive Presentation

Sober, unemotional, inexpressive communication that is not warm or engaging is a huge service pet peeve of mine. Customers are not impressed or attracted to an uptight, super serious person with a "flat affect" when they are being served. A servant must be respectful, honorable, and serve with feelings! The consumer cares about efficacy and how the service is provided. A staff member that can deliver in a gregarious manner would be far superior to a super timid person with poor conversational social skills or indifferent attitude.

Bossy, Pushy, or Abrasive Presentation

On the other end of the spectrum, there is being bossy, barking orders, or being abrasive to or around the patient. Antagonism, anger, or any other negative emotion are all unacceptable because they work against the end goal of moving a patient from a negative experience to a positive experience. Listening to some abrasive, vile person would *not* add a positive experience. It is equally disruptive to our customer service agenda when two teammates become engaged in a power struggle or argument. It's negative, creating angst or a conflict in the area of the consumer.

Listening to the Patient vs. Talking about Yourself

A close cousin to being abrasive or bossy is the act of not listening. Particularly, trying to talk constantly without hearing a patient's needs and wants. A staff member who wants to talk only about themselves and tell everyone around them, including their patient, about themselves is self-centered. This is a negative trait, as it does not create a connection with the patient or take interest in the patient and their life. This should not be confused with a confident person who is engaging in normal, two-way dialogue and talking about themselves in a conversational manner. Getting your sessions jump-started by talking about your weekend or issues that are positive and interesting in your life is a great way to make a therapist relatable. Some people are obviously quieter and prefer not to share much personally, and those boundaries should be respected. However, the more you can shine the spotlight on them as a person and make them the "star of the show," the more they will feel valued and appreciated by you and your team. You should seek to be interested in the other person instead of trying to be interesting yourself.

A great drill to try with staff to train this activity is something I learned from a Breakthrough seminar called "The Flashlight Drill."[27] Put two people in a dark room, facing each other with flashlights. When one has a question they want to ask the other, they shine the light on them. When that person is done addressing the question, the light goes off and vice versa. Some people, who lack self-awareness, talk about themselves constantly without taking an interest in the other party. So, in The Flashlight Drill, they would essentially shine the light on themselves and then just keep talking in the dark room, not knowing that another person was standing there feeling left out—and in the dark.

Shine your light on others!

Wasting Their Time

In the same vein as making a patient wait longer than ten minutes, wasting the consumer's time is a negative act. Time wasting is an insidious act created unintentionally, simply by a teammate being unaware of the clock. It is unacceptable in all of its forms. Slow processing of paperwork at intake, slow movement in general to a patient request, wasting time when they want to pay their bill, wasting time waiting in the reception area, wasting time in a treatment room waiting for a therapist—these should all be avoided.

The team should make seamless transitions from one team member to another, with limited gaps of time in between. The consumer is aware that time is money, so wasted time is the purest form of disrespect—it is arrogantly saying to the consumer that our time is more important than theirs. There isn't a patient alive who wouldn't rather get scheduled in fifteen seconds and then get out the door to pick up their kid from school instead of waiting for fifteen minutes to get scheduled while their kid is standing outside the school alone. Please be considerate of others' time, as it truly is our most precious, unrenewable resource.

Never Assume Happiness

Assuming the patient is satisfied and happy is the kiss of death! Assuming how they feel without actually knowing is, really, self-deception. The absence of complaining does not equal satisfaction. Many husbands have failed miserably at this very thing with their wives. He assumes she's happy, but did he actually ask her?

In psychology there is a term called "cognitive dissonance" that states each person's brain, in order to avoid the pain of a brutal truth, tends to defer by creating baseless alternate endings. When one "assumes" another's beliefs, values, or opinions without actually asking, one engages in mind-reading—which never works very well. We deceive ourselves into believing everything is sunshine, when in fact a severe thunderstorm could be on the way. We don't know either way, because we aren't willing to face the facts.

Any time two individuals engage with each other, there is a very complex cascade of neurophysiological responses that happen instantly to create or inhibit positive or negative feelings in one or both parties. Needless to say, one's emotional psychology can be a bit volatile and change in a second. Assuming is not equal to knowing.

What one person finds acceptable, the next patient will not. Each patient's needs, wants, tolerances, and patience levels are different, and they're different from day to day within each patient. A patient who had a great session on Friday will invariably be sore after the weekend. Do not assume that whatever great feelings you and "Friday patient" shared will be there with "Monday patient." Safe to say, you should *never* assume a patient is happy and satisfied with their care and service today simply because they were happy yesterday. The only way to be certain of a patient's satisfaction is by inquiring and communicating.

It is acceptable to ask and check on the patient's comfort repeatedly throughout every session to ensure you are on the right treatment path for them. It is *not* acceptable to ignore them and assume that because they haven't complained, that they are happy. It is also *not* acceptable to ask repeatedly in a fearful, apprehensive tone or posture as if you are expecting them to be uncomfortable or to dislike their treatment. Sounding like a droning, broken record is not OK. Just make sure you provide several check-ins, like a restaurant manager checking on tables, with a specific set of questions that require the consumer to actually provide a thoughtful response. Questions such as, "Are you doing okay?" might not provide enough substance for them to answer. A more appropriate question like, "What do you feel right now with this exercise?" will give you more indication of how they are truly doing.

The Only Two Guarantees to Quality

There are only two trusted methods I know of that guarantee a high perception of care. First, each individual staff member must be present with each patient and treat them like they are the most important person in the building at the time. Being present means truly focusing on them and giving them your undivided attention. One must be aware of one's surroundings, yet not lose focus. This truly is a challenging separator between professionals and amateurs: the ability to focus on your craft and execute it to the best of your ability, despite any distractions. Second, the team must be in a constant mode of quality assessment, ensuring that each patient treatment session exceeds 100 percent in quality. The two methods are very simple, yet they are not easy.

The Five Senses: Leading Client Perception

For your employees to reach a skill 1 high-quality perception of care, they need to learn the fundamental basics for each of the five senses since the consumer will perceive their physical world through these senses. Our goal in The Feel-Good Experience is to stimulate *all* of the patient's senses through **sight, hearing, touch, smell,** and **taste.**

Sight

You and your team have to positively *show* care so that a patient can *see* it. Patients need to *see* an environment that is pleasing to the eye, such as a clean, well-groomed, well-dressed, professional staff. An orderly, bright, and balanced décor provides balance and visual stimulation when paired with pleasing, soothing colors—such as blues, greens, yellows, and earth tones. Cleanliness, updated décor, and order show "professionalism," "attention to detail," and "an attitude of excellence" to the client's eyes.

The client should *see* dynamic, positive interactions between team members and between other patients and the team. The way people treat each other is a catalyst for how the environment and the culture of the organization will end up being. If everyone is pleasant, emotionally controlled, professional, and hardworking, patients will see this culture first hand. That alone will speak more boldly about quality and customer service than any marketing brochure ever could.

They should also *see*, clearly, an organized, controlled flow of care. Your team should be escorting patients, working swiftly through the process effectively and efficiently, and directing a clean, crisp beginning and end to the process. An obvious cycle creates comfort and stability. A chaotic environment does not breed feelings of peace, comfort, relaxation, or trust like an organized, swift, definable environment does. Balance and order bring harmony and peace to a patient receiving care; they are tenets of calmness and serenity that can aid in the patient's healing journey, but they can only be seen by the patient if customer service presentation becomes an integral part of the team's culture.

It can't be fake, forced, or inconsistent—it must be in each staff member in how they carry themselves, what they think about, their attitudes, and their verbal, vocal, and body-language communication skills. As previously covered, if a staff member lacks the alignment of what they are saying, how they are saying it, and what their posture and body awareness are saying, they will lack trust and credibility with the patient. A patient who does not buy into the provider's recommendations will usually fail to do so based on a failure of the therapist's or staff members' abilities to deliver a proper customer service presentation of the highest quality.

Hearing

All teammates have to speak in a controlled, positive, intentional manner at all times. They have to intend for the patient to *hear* them being positive, uplifting, fun, and enjoyable.

"Playing Catch"

Being able to understand "intentional communication," whether speaking or listening, is like playing catch with a baseball. The thrower gets the attention of the catcher to ensure they are ready and aware, then throws the ball directly to them. They don't toss the ball short of them or over their head—they throw the ball directly *to* them. That is how intentional speaking is. The person catching says, "I got it," to acknowledge, then returns the ball by throwing it back in exactly the same manner: directly *to* the original thrower.

And that is how proper communication should be: get attention by looking at the person with eye contact, acknowledge each other, then speak clearly and with a proper volume, as if you are throwing your voice and your words directly *to* them. Throw directly, not superhard or supersoft, but a direct throw to the chest of each recipient.

Nearly all customer service failures in healthcare (or any other industry) are from misunderstandings. That includes poor communication, where people weren't heard because they mumbled, or because they assumed the person heard them and ignored them, and so on.

Speak with the intention to be heard! The customer, too, needs to feel heard. They need to feel led through a conversation, like they are a part of the process. They deserve to know exactly what is going on and what is yet to come. Lead always with the intention of removing confusion.

Good intentional speaking is clear, bold, direct, and not confusing to the recipient. This is a "direct throw."

Bad intentional speaking is quiet, garbled, mumbled, poorly enunciated, and leaves the recipient wondering if you were directing your words to them or to someone else. This is the "no-look pass" or the "poorly thrown ball that falls short." Your words never reached them as you intended. That is a failed communication and, ultimately, a failed customer service opportunity.

Customer service is all about communication and proper understanding between people. Do all you can to ensure you keep things simple, basic, and clear. Many times in PT settings, you will need to speak over a large group of patients and therapists, so projection is very important. If you are speaking to a patient and their family, you need to take the time to ensure that you follow communication rules with each and every one of the family members who are caring for their loved one. A therapist who can't make eye contact, mumbles, or speaks with too much unexplained medical jargon will quickly lose respect—and, eventually clients.

Touch

Touch is a very important aspect of the perception of care in PT. We have to be very careful and skilled at how we touch our patients. This can be a very serious issue if done incorrectly or inappropriately. Everything discussed in this section is to be done with the utmost professionalism. When touch is used correctly, it can be a very powerful tool for helping positively influence the patient and, ultimately, their perception of you and your care.

We can touch people in a professional manner or in a personal manner, much how a friend or family member may touch you. You may also employ a method of combined touch, which is the preferred method within The Feel-Good Experience. Shaking someone's hand in a greeting is a professional touch connection, but not very personal. However, shaking someone's hand while using your other hand to either grasp or touch their shoulder firmly—or to cover and reinforce your handshake—is a personal yet professional touch.

Placing a hand on someone's back or shoulder or providing a hug should *all* be done in a gender-appropriate manner. Masculine and feminine touch is important in establishing rapport. Guys tend to like a firmer touch; girls tend to prefer a softer touch. Obviously, the personality and comfort level of the patient and the therapist plays a big role here. A female athlete will tend to find a high five or fist bump appropriate, while the female executive in a power suit may not. There are no absolutes when it comes to touch, other than to make it professional and make it fit the person. Touch is very crucial to the patient's perception of care and cannot be forced or ungenuine, as patients *will* sense it.

Using a personal touch approach within treatment allows for a greater connection, to the extent you or the patient are not uncomfortable. This becomes important when performing hands-on treatments, such as massage, forms of manual therapy, or application of rehab equipment such as braces, taping, electrical stimulation, ultrasound, or laser.

A patient's perception of care is much greater when the therapist is willing to hold or touch the body part that is to be treated. Allowing the machine, equipment, or implement used in treatment to be the focal point of touch and connection to the patient is impersonal. The entire focus of improving the perception of care is to actually care and create the perception with the patient that we are comfortable and accepting of them, so much so that we are willing to share space and connection with them. Most people in our modern technological world are becoming more high tech and low touch, and this leads to a dissociation with the medical provider working with them. When at all possible, treatment should include touch, as it is a powerful form of communication and acceptance, which in turn builds relationship bonds that hopefully last a lifetime.

When touching, cradle, support, embrace, or encapsulate the patient's body part, as appropriate, by using the palm of your hand to firmly *connect* with the person. If you barely graze their skin or poke with your fingers and act uncomfortable with light touch, as if you are afraid to touch them, the patient will sense very quickly that you are uncomfortable. That alone destroys the perception of care from the patient's perspective. When you touch, act as if you are placing your palms onto a hot towel that just came out of the dryer, not like you are repulsed by cleaning lint out of the dryer. One method is done with comfort and feeling in mind, while the other is done as an act of utility.

All touch has to be done with the utmost personal and professional touch; otherwise, a patient gets treated like an object, machine, or body part instead of as a person. You can be "high tech" in your treatment of their pain or diagnosis, but don't forget to be "high touch" as well.

Taste

When was the last time your taste buds were stimulated while at the doctor's office? Probably never, but when was the last time your taste buds were stimulated at a hotel reception counter? Many times, fresh cookies, mints, or coffee is present at a hotel front desk, but I have never seen them at a doctor's office counter before. Adding this component of sensation means one more opportunity to positively influence a person's perception of your company—or, in other words, it will give them a "taste" of your service quality!

Our facilities all have purified water stations near the reception area, as well as coffee, tea, and hot chocolate available. We also offer, on occasion, mints or treats, especially around holidays or special occasions. The added value we offer in these extras creates more opportunities to engage and talk with each customer to show how we are willing to serve them, versus simply sitting behind a desk and telling them to sit down and wait. We have always focused on shifting our service structure from a strictly "healthcare only," serious environment to one of enjoyment, and the coffee, water, and treats are a small offering with a big effect.

Moreover, it's not enough to have the coffee or water available, but it's the extra effort of our fetching it for them exactly to their liking. It's more about our asking them if they would like something to drink and then promptly delivering it to them in service. Again, where most clinics don't offer anything other than paperwork, we believe in an environment that mirrors the hospitality industry. If our focus is to make them comfortable and to meet any particular need or want they have at the moment, we increase our chances of having higher patient satisfaction, due to the added value offered.

Smell

All of us have been in an elevator, bus, or airplane with an unpleasant odor. A bad smell can totally ruin your experience, no matter how good the product or service was. I will never forget one night I took my family to one of our favorite pizza places. This place had amazing food, fast service, and reasonable prices. This one particular night, we were seated at a table closest to the restrooms when they had an unfortunate "plumbing incident." The smell was horrendous, and no matter how hard we tried to ignore it and enjoy our meal, we couldn't. We became nauseated and eventually had to leave. The psychological impact of that experience was so profound that my family refused to ever go there again, even though it was one of our favorite places and our displeasure had absolutely nothing to do with their food whatsoever.

This is how important the sense of smell can be to perceiving a pleasant experience or a rotten experience. Ultimately, maintaining a clean facility is the first step in having a nice-smelling service area. After every individual exits a personal treatment room or the gym area, we should always ensure that we disinfect and deodorize to neutralize any bad odors.

The smell of coffee and mild food smells can be pleasant alone, which we incorporate in our service offerings. However, sometimes when patients are in a lot of pain and under duress from other physical stressors, food, body odor, perfumes, or other aerosol scents can be enough to overstimulate the senses and make the experience unpleasant. Maintaining a neutralized, odor-free environment in our clinics is ideal.

Mentality

If all of the above senses (sight, hearing, touch, taste, and smell) are positive, pleasant stimulations, then we will have a positively stimulated patient or consumer.

All senses help us live our lives and experience our world, but in our physical therapy clinics, sight, hearing, and touch are the most commonly used senses. Therefore, the impact is greater when we focus more attention on these three senses as it pertains to targeting perceived care.

Perceived care is not an exact science, so it can't be scripted perfectly. However, you can automate, to some degree, a positive experience by consistently targeting patients' five senses. This automation removes the guesswork and the inefficiency of relearning what to do or say or how to behave with each person who comes in the door. Systematic Automation is the force that allows you to implement these perceived-care skills. It will also help you improve your skills repeatedly with every client to provide the best customer service experience possible.

Key Skills and Focal Points

Let Them Be Who They Are

The most pivotal customer service skill is the ability to remove all prejudices, beliefs, judgments, preconceptions, and images and just allow the customer in front of you to be who they are.

According to Dr. Thomas Harris, author of the bestselling self-help book *I'm OK-You're OK*, simply keeping a healthy balanced mindset about ourselves and others can remove limits and cognitive distortions.[28] For example, let's say you have successfully operated your front desk by maintaining *perfect* timing on your schedule, and as long as everybody makes their appointment exactly on time, you can keep your day running smoothly and efficiently. All it takes is one patient to come in five minutes late to ruin your *perfect schedule*. When that happens, you immediately run the pre-programmed application in your mind and you automatically *react* as such: you get angry, seeing how they single-handedly destroyed your perfect schedule for the day. You think, How dare they? Who do they think they are to be so irresponsible and foolish? You used to really like this patient. They were one of your favorites, but now you have all but written them off as a poor-character person, and you have now labeled them irresponsible and lazy.

So in a matter of minutes, you have gone from a well-respected, totally calm, happy professional who is in control to a raving-out-of-control lunatic. The subconscious mind is very good about teaching us how to avoid pain or teaching to defend us from pain whether real or imagined. The action of the patient coming in five minutes late was definitely real. The over-reaction to the fifteen different scenarios that you played out in your mind for the next few hours and how much pain and torment this person and people like them have caused others is not real.

This is a very extreme example, but this is how all prejudices, or mistreatment of any one, gets started and can transpire.

Instead, use I'm OK, you're OK self-talk, as previously mentioned with every person you encounter. Literally, this just means say and think of yourself as OK while also looking at a patient and saying they are OK also. When you do, your thinking becomes less charged, less imbalanced, and more available to accept people as they are. It's nearly impossible to communicate clearly with an individual that you judge with some hidden bias. Whereas, operating with a balanced mindset and belief about a patient or customer should establish a balance of respect for the person you are dealing with.

After all, if you are uncomfortable or simply dislike the person you are working with, don't you think they can sense it? They can!

In essence, lead yourself and seek to find something positive, or at the very least accepting, about every person you are servicing. That will guarantee your mind and thoughts are directed toward positive intentions with the customer, thus furthering the high perception of care and service.

100 Percent Improvement and Satisfaction Is the Number One Goal

In The Feel-Good Experience, we use two very simple key tools to quickly gauge how well or how poorly a patient is doing in treatment: the pain-analog scale and a percentage-improvement scale.[29]

First, we ask every patient at every single session to rate their pain that day on a zero-to-ten scale—zero being no pain and ten being an ER visit. Then, we immediately use past measurements to bring the patient into remembrance of where their previous scores were.

Most patients are prone to the negative, so no matter how great a product or service can be, our minds will tend to "downplay" it and/or find a negative bias. In most cases, this negative bias is not fact; however, whatever a customer's perception is, is what we use as our yardstick for a great experience.

So, for instance, a patient who had improved from an eight down to a five on the pain scale after just one week of PT is now in a bad mood, so they tell you that they are back to an eight pain level. Your immediate response should be to find any piece of data you can use to retrain or redirect their minds to what is truthful. For instance, you could say, "So, you are telling me that your pain is as bad as it was when you started PT? Are you sure? Because you walked in without a limp and actually reported to me that you were feeling much better with walking?"

You need to be their cheerleader. And when you do, generally, the patient will "go inside their mind's eye" and recalibrate, and then return with a comment of, "Oh yeah, you're right. It's much better." They will fill in the blanks of all the things they can do now that they couldn't before! By getting the patient to confess and verbalize positive outcomes, they will retrain their mind and perceptions toward the positive.

Now, you may come across the stubborn client who crosses their arms and insists, saying, "No. You're wrong. My pain is at an eight!" What do you do then?

You can't argue with someone who won't accept logic. If they are walking better and moving faster, then they *are* better! We have had this many times, with someone who has had chronic pain forever, or someone who truly wants to be ill and refuses to accept that they are better. We don't let up. We refuse to give in to failure. They *are* better—it's measurable and clearly observable— so your job is to make them believe it, because it's true. We *drag* a lot of patients across the finish line. We provide the strength and stamina for them to finish the race, even when they don't think they have the strength to finish.

In order to achieve this number one goal of improvement and satisfaction, we must do these drills daily with every patient, with the family members who bring them in, and with anyone who can affect that patient's perception of care.

Improvement or "Betterment" Is the Number Two Goal

We strive to "drag every patient across the finish line" in our model because in some cases, we believe in their success more than they do. As leaders in this model, we should believe in our abilities and their abilities to reach success.

However, while we believe everyone can improve, realistically, some patients won't get to 100 percent improvement. In those moments, we should not focus on the physical outcomes but instead, seek to drive a focus toward "betterment."

Get the client to realize that the reason they are better is because of the efforts of you and the organization. If a patient with a twenty-year history of chronic pain reports 80 percent improvement, that might be a huge win for that patient considering what they have been through. Make sure that they give you and your organization credit for their betterment. Make sure they say their improvement isn't because of meds, their doctor, their chiropractor, their diet, or whatever else they will try to assign the credit to. Always, always, always redirect their minds to the positive and connect that positive with you and your organization.

Remember, perception of care is all about what they perceive, sense, think, feel, and ultimately, believe the level of care was. To have a high perception of care, they have to know who *really* got them better.

Ensure They Perceive Quality Care

We all can get comfortable, complacent, or super busy at times, and our quality delivery and customer service skills can decline or become placid. When a patient starts cancelling or no-showing, that is a clear red flag. If they are choosing a salon appointment over you or rearranging their PT appointments around other things in their life, you are not a priority in their life. You, as a therapist, should be aware at all times of how the patient feels about your quality delivery. They should perceive the value of PT as greater than what they could get at a gym or fitness facility, or on their own with a home program.

Unfortunately, many physicians who believe that PT is expensive and drives up the high cost of healthcare validate their patient's belief that they can just do it at home. In fact, PT composes less than 2 percent of the US Healthcare GDP. Doctors who once were referring to PT are now handing over exercise brochures and educational pamphlets under the guise of "physical therapy." As insulting as this may be to the physical therapy profession, it is nonetheless fact.

We have become a commodity, like breakfast cereal. For the most part, there is nothing special about Raisin Bran. Kellogg's, Post, and many other brands make their version of it. Nobody is going to drive across Manhattan to get a box of Post Raisin Bran—they will just buy the generic brand at the corner store. Now, if the same guy is trying to buy a Ferrari, chances are he *has* to drive across Manhattan to find the dealer that can actually sell them.

World-renowned surgeons and hospitals are like Ferraris, *not* commoditized, but PT is more like Raisin Bran. You can get chiropractic, PT, and massage therapy from anywhere, and it generally appears to be all the same. What we do is the same— but how we do it isn't!

In order to separate and stand out from the other PTs and the other professionals out there, we *have* to provide a five-star customer service experience that delivers a WOW factor and leaves a lasting, positive sensation in the customer.

Testimonials

Lay the groundwork for the patient so the patient can't wait to write their success story about their experience. To recap, the groundwork consists of:

- creating a positive, energetic environment around them
- being present with them
- listening intentionally

- communicating intentionally
- asking key questions about their recovery (such as the pain scale and the percentage improvement scale)
- answering any questions that they may have
- anticipating any need they may have
- treating them like a guest in your house
- keeping them moving through the process
- not wasting their time
- and making their time in the clinic the most valuable use of their time

If you do everything I've taught you leading up to this moment so far, a good testimonial should be no problem.

The questions "Are you one hundred percent better? What successes have you had? What wins have you had?" should open up the patient to exactly what they need to write a success story or a testimonial. Most patients are shy, introverted, self-deprecating, and aren't writers. Let them express whatever they want—it's the emotions you are looking for, and you want all the emotions to be positive. Whatever they express emotionally to you is what you want to capture. Their experience should be one that is so emotional and expressive to them that they desire to write a story. This is so vital because this will be the lasting feeling they will have toward you and your team.

We believe in making a celebration out of patient graduations when they finish care. We get the testimonial, and we provide all the touch, hugs, smiles, conversation, and laughter we can. We then provide the patient with a parting gift from our clinic merchandise, such as a t-shirt, coffee mug, etc. The most important thing is to make sure your final moment is a home-run experience!

Chapter 3

Skill 2: Create Positive Moments through Stations and Zones

erceived care is the fuel that propels The Feel-Good Experience. The clinic stations and zones are the actual mechanical machine that gets fueled by the high level of perceived care.

Five stations make up the step-by-step logistics, like bases to reach on a baseball diamond. This entire five-station process only works if each and every station is positive and focused on delivering their product quickly and effectively.

Any "let down" from one station affects the entire "station loop." Thus, any let down at any station is like pouring water on the fire we are trying to start.

The zones, like in baseball, refer to any area surrounding a teammate at any given time, much like outfielders and infielders covering a particular area or "zone of responsibility." In baseball, any ball hit into a fielder's particular zone should never get past them—and if it does, another teammate should overlap into that zone to help make the play. So too, we have zones in our clinics which act as a safety net, ensuring service is provided in each station and no "dropped or missed balls" occur in customer service.

Station 1: Front Desk/Reception

The front desk is the first encounter and first impression any customer will have. The receptionist is like a catcher in baseball; they are the beginning of the entire customer service operation. They must be the spark that ignites the process. If the environment is dead quiet, depressing, solemn, serious, or focused on clerical tasks, the customer will *immediately* perceive a slow, unengaging, negative environment upon entering. The more negative or neutral the beginnings are, the more effort it takes from the team to lift that patient up emotionally, mentally, and psychologically in order to counter their first "taste" of the practice environment.

Thus, the individuals running this station *must* have a high level of friendliness, extroversion, and social skills. Human beings attract and react positively to those who are positive and kind. A receptionist who is more of a task-master or a computer software expert is better off somewhere else. Instead, you want people who have strong social skills and can strike up a conversation with anyone, as well as having the typical receptionist skills, like managing a schedule and keeping organized.

If the receptionist is shy or cannot initiate action, then they will struggle with this role. If one struggles to make conversation, a cheat sheet of topics can always be implemented, including top-ics such as weather, employment, hobbies, family, and weekend plans. Have the receptionist make notes and follow up with the person the next time they see them.

The person who likes to socialize, likes people, likes to talk, and loves to make things fun is the perfect candidate for this aspect of customer service.

Reception Skill 1: The Ability to Face Someone Comfortably

This is a prerequisite one needs to master before one can excel at any other aspects of this station. If you can't face someone comfortably, how could you possibly lead, influence, schedule, communicate, negotiate, or build a relationship? All that is nec-essary at the receptionist station, and it starts with being totally self-assured and comfortable facing people.

If you are a person who struggles with shyness, introversion, or self-esteem challenges, try this drill to help you overcome face-to-face issues: two people face each other and look each other in the eye. The object is to stay in this state of focus, looking them in the eye, until you shift from feeling anxious, nervous, emotional, and uncomfortable, to feeling totally calm and at peace, all while still looking the person in the eye.

This can be done either with customers, coworkers, friends, or anyone willing to participate. It can feel awkward at first, but the longer you perform the drill, the more you begin to relax and become present and mindful about merely looking at someone and being comfortable in their space. You are not looking at them in judg-ment, but in acceptance—and in acceptance of yourself, as well.

If, throughout the drill, you continue to be uncomfortable, then you must start with a gradient approach. Start with facing some "thing" as opposed to a person. Then progress to looking at something about a person—such as their ear or nose—then ultimately specifically look them in the eye. You must be able to be present and face customers as they come in if you plan on exceeding customer service expectations. An advanced skill is looking someone in the eye while they are talking without being self-conscious about looking them in the eye. If you keep getting in your headspace and feeling anxious about facing people, keep practicing. It definitely gets better with time. Eventually, it becomes automatic, and when you get to that skill level, you can start communicating strongly and confidently, because your nonverbal communication is stable and strong.

Receptionist Skill 2: Ability to Connect to People

Once you can comfortably face someone, you need to connect with them. To do that, the receptionist needs to get to know the patients. The receptionist must take a sincere interest in every person, not only as a customer but as a human being, by finding them interesting on some level. It is critical to building rapport to better lead and service the patient throughout their time in the clinic. A true, professional receptionist doesn't view a relationship with a patient as a task but as an opportunity. They enjoy getting to know everyone's name and learning something of interest about them. Then those who are good at their craft will use this information repeatedly in every encounter with that person. This repeated connection makes us more like a family or a community than just a healthcare office. And believe me, since there is nothing attractive, fun, or exciting about a healthcare office, you need a good receptionist and customer support so patients look forward to coming instead of dreading their visit. This fact of relationship building and connection is why every encounter must start with a smile and a positive greeting.

Receptionist Skill 3: Positive Greetings

The ideal receptionist must have a vocal tone that sounds like music: bright, bold, loud but not obnoxious, and with clear enunciation. When in doubt as to what a clear, positive voice should sound like, listen to a radio announcer or TV show host.

The receptionist must engage and grasp each and every person who comes in the door with their presence, intention, and emotion, and they must do it through the first encounter, as the first encounter is what sets the tone for their experience that day. Their voice should be magical and musical to positively move the person. A voice that is lighthearted, interested, assertive, clear, concise, and positive with no mumbling is perfect.

Optimism, charisma, and a spirit of inspiration and hope must be sensed by the patient and their family as they enter the reception area. Think of a time you entered a fun, lighthearted room or event. Contrast that with one that was heavy, dark, and negative. Ideally, we seek to have our clinic's positive environment so strong you can feel it from the parking lot. Emotional tone and spirit drive that sensation. The more a patient feels a strong vibe of positivity, the greater experience overall they will have.

A simple, "Hey, Bob, it's great to see you today!" or "What do you think about that weather?" can be just the right stimulus to get the spark started.

If you have a hard time making small talk and basic conversation, there are many good books and articles on the art of conversation. If you remember from the previous chapter, it's not so much *what* we say but more *how* we say it. Your vocal tone and body language will emit more control and influence than the words that you say.

You will encounter Negative Nancys and Debbie Downers, but *never* allow negativity to derail your initiatives. You are positive... period! You are going to respect and honor and make the day of the person in front of you, whether or not they choose to agree with you for the moment. All you can control is yourself. Keep being positive! Keep running the drill exactly as it's written, and eventually, you *will* make a difference in that person's life, and they will evolve and start to change.

It is a fact that a negative person can't handle being in the presence of positivity forever, so they will either quit altogether, or they will start adjusting their behavior.

This was shown when I analyzed twenty-one years' worth of statistics, tallying cancellations, no-shows, and drop-offs from our caseload. I concluded that 2 percent of our entire caseload of attrition is due to bad patient attitudes, such as chronic mental illnesses where they self-sabotage, etc. That means that only *2 percent of the time* does a person quit because they can't stand the positive, caring nature and winning attitude of our team. It always behooves us to keep applying positivity and leading them with our best, each and every day.

It will change their lives and it will change yours. Helping a fellow human being through one of the most difficult times of their life is not something to brush off as insignificant. You were an important part of that moment for them. There is very little in life that is quite as fulfilling.

Reception Skill 4: Hosting a Reception

Let's return to the title of receptionist. Receptionists are, in all actuality, a host of a reception—a host of a party! To have a "reception" is to have a "party" and "receive" people, such as in a wedding reception. So, you have to make it a party. Thus, after check-in, the receptionist should shift to creating a "fun and friendly" atmosphere in the reception area. To control the atmosphere in the reception area, much like a party host, the receptionist should make sure everybody is interacting. The receptionist gets the party going by greeting everybody and facilitating introductions. They should try to include everyone, and introducing people is the way to ensure that the atmosphere will take on a positive life of its own, one that won't require the receptionist to be constantly "working the crowd" like a comedy club. The best receptionists can get everyone in the reception area entertaining themselves, and then they can step away to work on something else and check in if necessary.

If patients in the reception area are shy, angry, or challenging in some way, it will take a strong, confident extrovert to get discussion topics and positive energy building back up again, and to get everyone involved relaxed and shifted back to a positive emotional environment.

At the very least, a receptionist should make a connection by offering coffee and then making sure, if they have to get back to their desk, that another teammate steps in to fill their void in the reception area. Someone should always be covering the reception area, not only for service and experience but for safety and liability management.

After this friendly atmosphere in reception, the customer will already be buzzing with positivity and moving toward a great experience by the time they are ready to be hosted to treatment.

Reception Skill 5: Verbal Reassurances

Control at the front desk comes from the receptionist's body language, internal confidence, and verbal skills. Verbally being in control and keeping the consumer invested and happy in their therapy *is* the job. No matter how much engagement and conversation one partakes in, eventually, the patient is going to have irritations. These irritations occur with long waits, especially if they are in pain, are uncomfortable, or have some other problem on their mind that is taking their energy.

Sometimes when you ask how they are getting along with their ailment or their therapy, you will receive a negative or unhappy response. No matter what the response, *always* redirect to a sense that everything will be all right. Reassure them that if they stick with their therapy (and definitely speak about their issues to their therapist), we will get it figured out and will do everything in our power to help them.

When you say these phrases, they must come from your heart, not your mind. The mind produces words, the heart produces the feeling that comes with the words through body language and the vocal tone. One thing you *never* want to relay is a message of pity or groveling about their problems. Hardships and trials in life are assumed, and PT is specifically a business that specializes in life's hardships and trials. However, our position and number one focus is to lead them out of their debilitated state, and that will be done emotionally, mentally, and spiritually.

Statements like "Oh, you poor thing. It sounds like you aren't doing well at all. I sure hope you can get some relief" should be avoided. Language that implies or assigns a victimhood state will not be tolerated, as that makes it acceptable for them not to take responsibility for improving their condition. A culture of sympathy, pity, blaming, and victimhood suppresses the human spirit and suffocates the healing process. The first step toward achieving anything is mental, so allowing a patient to feel sorry for themselves and then accentuating their pathetic and powerless state is cruel and unethical, in my opinion.

Instead, we encourage positive, life-filled, yet realistic language such as: "I understand you are feeling down about your condition; that is totally normal. Please believe me when I say that if you will keep sticking with your therapy and doing your best, you will see improvement. Every patient who comes in here experiences and says exactly the same thing you're saying right now. Every one of those past patients on our Wall of Fame (pointing to our wall of testimonials and pictures) struggled at first and didn't believe things would improve, but they all eventually turned the corner and started getting better."

One key automated statement should definitely be in your receptionist's arsenal: "We will be right with you," or "We'll get you back just as soon as we can."

The receptionist should check on patients in reception every two to three minutes and communicate with the aides or therapist to see if they can expedite the process. If, by chance, the wait is beyond five minutes, then be prepared to really keep the atmosphere lighthearted, fun, and enjoyable (please see receptionist skill 3: Hosting A Reception). The distraction of something positive, such as interesting conversation, laughter, or a discussion about current event topics or weather occupies those open thoughts in one's mind that can otherwise wander toward the uncomfortableness of sitting and waiting. I have gathered significant proof over twenty years of implementation of this tactic that some wait times of almost twenty minutes were thought to have only been five or ten due to the fact that the client was simply enjoying themselves. Time flies when you're having fun, right?

Station 2: Host/Hostess

This station is almost entirely nonverbal communication and body language. The messages received by the patients either waiting in reception or being ushered to treatment are all from your body awareness, body position, use of touch, and vocal tone.

The host/hostess is considered a station simply because it contains a very powerful customer service ingredient due to the nonverbal presentation in the hosting tasks and techniques.

The host/hostess must have the self-awareness necessary to convey comfort with control, let the patient be who they are, and respect and honor them for who they are.

Japanese Culture of Service

The arts of honor and respect were demonstrated explicitly during my trip to Japan many years ago. I was immediately met with smiles from the flight attendants and the pilots, as if their lives were immediately brightened by having me on their flight to Tokyo. I was one out of probably two hundred people on this flight, yet they provided me a warm moist towel to freshen up before they served me drinks and dinner. They serviced me and made me feel valuable and special in a manner that I was honestly not accustomed to in the states.

My experiences of respect and honor in customer service continued as I traveled around the city. We walked toward a McDonald's, and we were met at the front doors with both doors opened for us by two workers dressed in typical McDonald's uniforms. They smiled and bowed at us as we walked through the doors. Then, upon ordering, the speed, cleanliness, and ease of the system were incredible. I was literally ushered in by a worker carrying my tray of food and was seated at a table, much like you would at an upper-end restaurant. I had many experiences that solidified in my mind that the Japanese culture had cornered the market on customer service.

My final experience of incredible service was before we traveled to the airport to go home again. We stopped at a gas station to fuel up for the trip. It was completely full service, with an attendant doing the fueling. After paying, several attendants went to the street and stopped oncoming traffic, then waved us onto the roadway to ensure we were safe. They were all bowing at us, honored with the opportunity to serve us as customers.

This "Japanese culture" approach is how the host/hostess station is ideally handled. The mindset one needs to take on is how to honor and respect someone as if you were bowing to them—without actually bowing. That is the secret to this position: the highest levels of respect and honor are granted to the customer.

The host/hostess should always start by smiling and greeting the patient by their name. They should offer a hand or support to them as necessary. This may look like a handshake, but in our office, it may likely involve steadying clients as they walk to their seat, or simply showing care and compassion in helping them get situated. Whatever level of service and help they need is what you want to offer.

Much like an usher in a theatre, auditorium, or stadium, the host/hostess not only directs or instructs the clients where to go, but actually leads them. Being led while receiving service in a business is a comforting action and an act that adds value.

Compare and contrast two scenarios. In the first, a patient is physically ushered to the area they need to be in for the next stage of their treatment, such as a treatment room, the gym for exercises, or the business office for financial and account information. In the second, they are merely pointed to where they need to go and given a litany of directions they are supposed to remember.

Being led and ushered to your destination is an act of caring and serving, as you are trying to give and support without assuming they know what to do or where to go. The service of ushering implies that we are in control, and we intend to help and assist you. Whereas, giving orders and directives to someone is an act of laziness and implies that you don't care or at least don't have enough ambition to get up and provide help in their time of need. It is very poor empathy and shows insensitivity to the customer who is specifically there for your help.

Host/Hostess Skill 1: The Walk and Talk

"The walk" is the most important aspect of this station. If you run far ahead of the patient or their family and create separation, your body language says, "I am impatient. You are slow, and I don't have time for this." It doesn't give anyone the warm and fuzzy feeling of someone walking *with you* and sharing the space together with conversation. In addition, if you allow the patient to take the lead and you fall behind them while they are intently walking to the treatment area, you give the impression that you aren't intentional about what you are doing and thus do not look professional, in charge, or like a leader.

To have the "right" walk:

Match speed and assistance to the person in whether they are a slow or fast walker and how much physical help they may need depending on their ailment and physical limitations.

Match and lead communication, such as matching and leading them with body language, vocal tone, and verbal conversation.

Match and lead with your personality. Keep it simple. What's their personality like? Are they a serious, straight-faced, "no-nonsense" type person? Or are they sociable, lighthearted, and smiling? Reframe your conversations, behaviors, and directions toward the type of person they are. Accept them as they are.

Know your destination. The presentation of not knowing is one of the worst images possible. Imagine being hosted to a table in a restaurant, only to be uprooted and moved afterward to a booth across the room. It removes the feeling of stability and certainty we all need. The more the host/hostess is aware of what they are doing and where they are actually leading the patient, the greater the confidence in the consumer about the system, processes, and team.

While ushering the patient or patient's family, you must read their body language. Are they open or closed off to you? Are they conversational? Are they happy or irritable? Are they "no-nonsense" or are they easygoing about their time in the clinic? All of these cues should be triggers to how you react and respond to them and how you host them back. A softer, more sensitive person might need a hand on the back for compassion, whereas a less sensitive, more direct person might simply need a handshake and direct travel to the treatment area. It's important to make a connection to who the person is and match them as close as you can. We all desire a mirror image of ourselves, whether we realize it or not, so the closer we can mirror the person we are ushering, the closer the connection will be, and thus the greater the experience.

Conversation during ushering is like polishing the product. It's that important. How many times have all of us been ushered in a service environment by someone who wouldn't talk to us? How did that make you feel? Personally, it makes me feel like a thing instead of a person. Our stations need to be gifted in the art of conversation and how to use it to advance the customer service experience.

Start with small talk, such as news, weather, sports, work, family, hobbies. Then branch off from there, and take notes. The best hosts are those who remember details about each person and build conversations around information gathering during "the walk." Each time, they build upon those intimate details, adding a positive feeling that the client is being related to, being heard, and being valued as a person, not just a diagnosis. This avoids a transactional feeling and moves toward an experiential feeling. That *is* THE FEEL-GOOD EXPERIENCE!

Host/Hostess Skill 2: The Ability to Face Someone Comfortably

This skill was a prerequisite in station 1 as well. You have to be able to look at someone before you can communicate with them. If you are uncomfortable looking or facing someone, how can you possibly greet them, read their body language, carry on a conversation with them, and lead them effectively? As the proverb says, "The eyes are the window into the soul." Eye contact is a critical skill to develop in order to become better at reading, analyzing, and predicting a person's behavior and personality. Tiredness, pain, remorse, depression, enthusiasm, happiness, irritation, attraction, repulsion, disagreement, and a multitude of other emotions can be determined simply by looking someone in the eye.

A host who avoids eye contact sends the wrong message of poor confidence, poor self-worth, and incompetence. If the receptionist has properly created feelings of confidence within a patient, the host can either strengthen those feelings of consumer confidence or destroy them based on how they use or avoid eye contact. The impact of eye contact when communicating is only as effective or ineffective as the host's ability to perform it comfortably without having to focus on the skill itself. The more energy it takes to focus on looking someone in the eye, the less energy one can devote toward listening skills, picking up nonverbal cues, and really, truly receiving the message the patient is sending.

Host/Hostess Skill 3: Granting Beingness and Respect

Granting a person "beingness" means simply to accept someone as they are. A nonjudgmental observation of someone without any prejudices is an easy way to build rapport—or to, at minimum, not create strife or repel the consumer.

Focus on the positives and eliminate the negatives. In practical terms, seek to find some characteristic that you like about someone. The mere act of focusing on someone's positives builds affinity and attraction between people to a point where they can sense it and feel acceptance. For example, if a person comes in who has on a pair of shoes you like, focus on the shoes and/or compliment them on their shoes. Even someone who can be abrasive or rude has some positive qualities, *if* you are willing to find and focus on them.

Prejudices only serve to highlight our differences in a negative way and push people apart, as opposed to unifying. Race, gender, socioeconomic status, appearance, orientation, and intelligence level are just a small sampling of ways in which we can find "rightness" or "wrongness" about another person. These prejudiced, judgmental, over-simplistic assumptions we make about people *never* serve either of our purposes well.

Think about a time in your past when you felt insecure, judged, and unaccepted. Then consider how nice it would have been to have had someone, in that moment, befriend you and accept you exactly as you were.

If someone is behaving oddly but not threateningly or dangerously, make a mental note then simply respect them. Allow them to be totally at ease and to be whoever they want to be in peace and without judgment.

No recommendations provided in this book should ever be taken out of context. Never lose common sense or refrain from using logic if you perceive danger. It is certainly better to exercise caution and judgment in those situations and to be wrong than to assume everyone loves one another and end up a victim of a violent crime.

Unfortunately, healthcare environments are increasingly becoming targets of violent crime. In the vast majority of situations, patients who enter your facility are there for the right reasons and are good, law-abiding citizens. They are who this rule of granting beingness and acceptance without prejudice applies to.

Host/Hostess Skill 4: Positive Uplifting Communication

The Feel-Good Experience is all about leading patients to a better state, physically, emotionally, mentally, and spiritually, through positive, uplifting communication. We should sound like a positive talk show host when we work with patients and service them.

Generically positive conversation should follow this three-step pattern: first is general topics, second is their interests, and third is how they are doing.

The art is not to ask the questions to get answers but to pick up clues about them as a person and then to build upon that in conversation. Ultimately, the goal is to build a relationship that will create a return client for life—and one who will refer their friends and family.

The actions of customer service should be experiential, not simply transactional!

Host/Hostess Skill 5: Proper Body Language[30]

This skill is built off the section earlier in the book that discusses verbal and nonverbal communication. All the individual body expressions we present to the consumer reveal our true heart's intent. If we are having a bad day and are focused on our negative thoughts, how do you suppose you sound when you greet a patient in the reception area?

Consider: Are you really smiling or just forcing a smile? If a smile is not genuine, it *will* be felt by the consumer or the recipient you are facing. You can't say, "It is so good to see you," and be believable when you dislike the person you are talking to. Your body posture, facial expressions, vocal tone, and volume—combined with the words—are what demonstrates credibility and believability. This is a skill to work on if you are not a great communicator. If you start with the basics of proper nonverbal posturing that universally speaks "positivity" and train these skills repeatedly, you will develop an improved self-awareness and a "kinesthetic awareness" about how your body feels when in these postures.

You will eventually train your body at a subconscious level that is automatic and becomes part of you. Communication delivery is an art form and is crucial to delivering great customer service.

Eye Contact: Maintain direct, yet comfortable eye contact to show your confidence. People who are trying to develop these skills for the first time are often super aware of trying to force eye contact. The result is a creepy or glaring stare. Obviously, the goal isn't to frighten or put the consumer on the defensive, so a great technique to fix that problem is to focus on only one eye of the individual while speaking with them.

You will be within ten feet or less when speaking to most people. Focusing on one eye keeps your pupils, at that close range, from darting side to side to view each eye. The more sensory information your eyes are trying to process can strain your eyes. Thus, if you focus on both eyes, it can also cause that creepy look of intense focus, as your eye becomes fatigued, therefore, losing pupillary control and lubrication. When your eyes dry out from a glaring, eyes-wide-open stare, you will start that subconscious repetitive blinking to produce tears and moisture. And now you are quite uncomfortable and not relaxed, and you are not truly focused on what the other person is saying. They will certainly sense the discomfort and agitation you will no doubt be experiencing.

This entire cascade of negativity can be prevented by picking one eye to focus on. Do this, and you will no longer be as anxious about speaking to people. You will, in fact, have improved confidence, effectiveness, and respect in your interpersonal relationships.

Head up and shoulders back: This is biomechanically a stable, stronger body posture. Not only does this position reduce fatigue by allowing your body to function with less effort but it also prevents the development of neck and shoulder pain. A professional, confident person does not slouch like a teenage boy slumping on a couch. Discipline yourself with self-speak, such as repeating

"Head up, shoulders back," upon entering a room or greeting someone. Avoid the slacker image of slouching by using these postural cues, as they will help paint the picture of a confident, strong professional with a great, attractive image of health and vitality to customers.

Calm, visible hands: Keep your hands apart from one another and in plain sight. The rule of keeping hands in plain sight eliminates nearly all negative issues that can arise with one's hands—such as crossing arms or folding hands together on one's lap, both of which imply insecurity and weakness.

Keeping hands where you can see them helps prevent talking too much with your hands, as this can be very distracting. Assertive hand gestures are appropriate when a political candidate uses them along with an energetic, determined speech. Wild hand gestures are not appropriate when that same political candidate is sitting across from one or two people in a small town coffee shop. Consistency, balance, harmony, and a system in alignment are what we seek in order to perfect our professional communication and presentation skills. I can't emphasize enough how important our presentation to others is, especially in customer service roles.

Keeping your hands in plain sight also prevents you from seeking comfort and security by sticking your hands in your pockets. This is particularly important on the first meeting. This is not an exact science, so these rules are qualitative, not quantitative. What works upon a first meeting, when everyone is nervous and getting established, are not the same rules for a relationship that has matured over years and years—which is our ultimate goal.

Palms should be open with no clenched fists, as that implies a readiness to fight. Walking around with fists ready to go is exhausting and a sure sign of internal stress and anxiety. Release the tension—release your fists!

Arms crossed upon first greeting implies defensiveness, irritation, or a lack of acceptance of the other person. As time passes, or in moments of deeper thought, problem solving, or professional work with the patient, it certainly becomes more important and acceptable to use the "arms crossed" posture. It is also an appropriate response upon hearing some challenging or emotional story that is being shared. However, during the first meeting, both parties are strangers, so to further the relationship in a positive manner, it would stand to reason that the parties would want mutual acceptance, openness, and inclusion. Therefore, crossed arms should initially be avoided.

Mirroring body language: Openness, inclusion, and acceptance are spoken nonverbally, often by mirroring the person you are talking to. Interestingly, there are some tweaks to this "mirroring rule" as it pertains to men and women, as well when it comes to ethnic differences, age differences, and when dealing with those with special needs or disabilities. The simplest rule to follow is to pay attention and be sensitive to how the individual is responding to you, your personal space, or your body position. Someone who is uncomfortable will continually be changing positions or adjusting their torso away from you to lessen the connection. Moreover, if you are not sensitive and respectful to boundaries, you will likely see a change in the patient's countenance or that of their family member or caregiver. Their decline in attraction will be palpable, and you will need to adjust your technique rapidly or risk losing a chance for a great relationship, which ultimately will negatively affect the patient's overall experience.

When it pertains to males and females—more specifically, masculinity and femininity—the genders will generally react in the following way:[31] When a man faces and communicates with another man, they will generally meet at a face-off with a firm handshake, mirroring torso to torso. Upon completion of the handshake, the two men will remain in a direct mirroring-image position, open to each other, through conversation. If one seeks something from another, like a business transaction, there is an automatic hierarchy established by either standing above them or putting a desk between them, showing their authority. Once the transaction has been completed, the two men are now "equals." Any further transactions or interactions from those two same men will generally happen at a 45-degree angle, shoulder to shoulder, as they communicate in a posture that is slightly moving away from each other.

I have seen this trend violated, and it usually gets tense and, at a minimum, verbally combative or argumentative. It has been explained that when a man faces off with another man as equals without giving an inch, they are preparing for a confrontation.

The opposite can be true between women and men in transactions. Men and women will generally face each other mirrored and never move from that posture—particularly if acceptance is met. A man generally will continue to face off when in disagreement or when unaccepting of what they are being told. A woman's body language is often face-to-face mirroring when even in a mild level of acceptance or agreement. As her acceptance or agreement increases, she will actually close the gap or distance of personal space. However, if she becomes disinterested, frustrated, in disagreement, or is outright angry or repelled, she will turn away and increase the distance from the other party.

Position yourself at their height: Position yourself openly but at a person's height. If a patient is in a wheelchair, I beg you not to stand over them and literally talk down to them. Always lower yourself from "upon high" to meet the person right where they are. Never lower yourself to another in a disrespectful, submissive, or self-deprecating manner, but lower yourself to another out of respect, honor, and power. From that equal position, respect and agreement are found and your leadership can begin.

Please do not try to force these tips or attempt to prove these tips. You will simply take someone who is uncomfortable and make them more anxious. Remember, your goal is to always be serving, selling, and leading the consumer to an amazing experience. A great customer experience can't happen if the customer is forced to be uncomfortable or anxious. If you pay attention to their body language and cues, you will quickly pick up on their "tells," like a poker player. Then you can lead them to a more comfortable place, whether it's simply you backing off, slowing down your speech to reduce the anxious energy generated, or offering them a seat if appropriate.

In all things, you want to be confident and assertive, but certainly not aggressive or intimidating. If you intend to build a relationship, accept the person, and make them feel comfortable, then try to avoid anything that might make them feel unaccepted, intimidated, or unincluded.

There is an entire field of research devoted to reading body language and the tendencies of people to give you clues about what people are *really* saying to you. There is no way we can cover that entire field of study in this book, but I would encourage anyone who wants to improve their customer service skills, sales skills, or people skills, in general, to study and apply some of these references. The *real* messages we are all sending are in our nonverbals!

Station 3: Treatment/Caregiver

The third station in The Feel-Good Experience process is the station of treatment or the caregiver. This is any customer service action that occurs within the technical treatment of the patient, whether it is the setup by a PT tech or the actual care provided by a therapist. The same rules apply here: it is about how the treatment is completed and perceived by the patient and has nothing to do with how *the therapist* feels about the care they delivered.

Remember, the patient doesn't care about a therapist's schooling, their credentials, their class placement, or whether or not the therapist adheres to a "McKenzie" or a "Mulligan" approach to spine treatment. The patient cares about physical results! That is why The Feel-Good Experience is superior as a customer service model in physical therapy delivery.

The Main Event

The caregiver station is where the *main party* should be happening! It starts at station one at reception but should be at its peak during the treatment at station three. This is where a lot of the five senses or components of perceived care get used constantly between all of the caregivers. Communication between all caregivers and patients should be very professional and respectful, yet fun! This station should incorporate listening to patients' needs and changes in symptoms, specifically changes in attitudes or perceptions of each patient each session.

The team should ensure that all guests are receiving attention. In a team-oriented treatment environment like this, it matters not whose caseload any patient is on, as they are all our patients and we all should all be keeping watch and attention on any guest in our house. This crossover has proven to be very effective in surpassing high expectations of a great experience.

Under this model, nobody in the clinic should be left alone at any given time. No one should be ignored, and everyone should be included in the fun party!

Technical Skills

Flowsheets, checklists, or recipes
These tools are sometimes scoffed at within the physical therapy profession. There is a belief that using checklists creates a culture of rote repetition where all clinical decision making is removed. However, when running clinic treatment processes, I have found checklists to be an invaluable tool in efficiency and consistency. It shortens a patient's time in the clinic, as well as provides immediate team-wide communication. It is a quick, effective delivery of the patient's treatment. Sometimes the simplest actions and tools create the biggest impacts in customer service.

Warmup/core treatment/cooldown
Establishing and adhering to this three-phase structure-of-care protocol ensures that we follow systematic consistencies from therapist to therapist and patient to patient. Specifically, each person on the team, whether therapist, aide, or receptionist will know what the general first step of the process will be: a warmup. They may not know the specifics, but this consistency provides the perception of team quality and competency.

Treatment Caregiver Skill 1:
The Ability to Face Someone Comfortably

This is a previously discussed skill but is still the prerequisite of communicating and addressing customers—and anyone. You must be able to face someone without being uncomfortable before you can effectively work with them. This is foundational before any other skills can be applied.

Treatment/Caregiver Skill 2:
Granting Beingness and Respect

This is, again, the ability to allow and accept someone for who they are without judgment or prejudice and just be present with them. This is crucial to establishing rapport with a patient and building trust. The necessity to accept all different personality types, opinions, genders, races, and any other category is critical.

This skill is more of an "attitude" than it is a task to perform. Granting beingness and respect means conveying the mindset of "I am okay, and I believe you are okay." "I am confident in who I am and I love myself, but I do not believe I am better than you, and I don't believe you are better than me." We share this place, this space, and this time together equally and respectfully.

This is the groundwork for building a relationship with a patient for life. By making them feel like they are valuable, appreciated, and respected, you have a greater chance of winning over the customer and leading them toward the experience you desire.

Treatment/Caregiver Skill 3:
Positive, Uplifting Communication

As in all stations, the caregiver *must* deliver a strong, confident, optimistic level of communication intentionally. Starting generally and progressing on a gradient with positive levels of communication, the therapist should ensure that each question-and-answer dialogue with the patient is always positive and constructive. A limiting, negative, pessimistic conversation or short-worded answers tend to limit the patient's openness and trust with the therapist.

The Feel-Good Experience is about having an optimistic attitude of leadership that uses empathy, kindness, compassion, and concern. We are building a culture around leading language that expects nothing but positive outcomes. Perfection is not attainable, but improvement and acceptance are. Realistic, believable, achievable *improvement* is what TFGE is all about.

We understand a patient's frailty and their tendency toward depression and hopelessness. Dealing with an emotionally fraught patient is not generally within the comfort zone of most therapists. More times than I can count, I have seen therapists freeze up like a deer in headlights because they were so uncomfortable with an upset patient.

I have also heard therapists and staff say very inappropriate, unhelpful, and actually discouraging things while a patient was upset, such as, "Look, I have told you and shown you what is wrong with you. The reality is, I don't know if you are going to run marathons or play sports again. We just need to get you scheduled three times per week for the next four weeks to get your function back."

The entire time the therapist was talking to this patient, the therapist was completely oblivious that he was talking to them with all mechanical logic like a robot, while they were trying to process the pain, anguish, suffering, and potential future of not being able to do what they loved. The therapist's blunt comments could have waited for another time since they did nothing to improve the bond between the therapist and patient and certainly did nothing to add value to the patient's outcome or experience.

So instead, remember positivity. Creating a free, trustworthy, and optimistic dialogue means the relationship has a better chance of growing, and that increases the chances of the customer not only receiving a great outcome but wanting to return in the future.

Treatment/Caregiver Skill 4: Proper Body Language

Nonverbal communication makes up most of our individual communication. Every patient encounter *has* to begin with a strong, positive communication skill. As discussed previously, these are the basic body language cues that a caregiver can adjust daily to ensure that their communication skills are improving, thus improving their customer service skills:

- **Direct eye contact** relays confidence.
- **The head-up, shoulders-back position** elevates posture and provides an image of strength.
- **Maintaining an open body position and mirroring their body language** implies acceptance and furthers trust.
- **Having your hands free,** not in pockets and not crossing your arms, implies openness and security.

Treatment/Caregiver Skill 5: Positive Touch

Bringing many facets of perceived care together into one action would be using positive, professional touch communication. This action must convey the message, "I will take care of you, and you are in good hands." This, of course, can't happen without self-confidence. Once strong self-esteem is established, you will seem believable and trustworthy to the patient.

Always position the patient gently and appropriately using pillows, chairs for comfort and support, draping, and privacy. Use the highest level of perceived care with all gestures, movements, positioning, touch, and treatment.

Ultimately, how touch is done is TFGE difference. If you simply grab a patient's leg and move it around without talking to them first, it is a bit intrusive and inappropriate. You would be manipulating their leg as an attachment to the patient, not treating their leg as the *patient itself*. It's all about *how* we approach the patient with touch, communication, and professionalism.

Treatment/Caregiver Skill 6: Playing Zone versus Man to Man

The "garden variety" physical therapy clinic in the US utilizes a one-on-one approach to patient care. In contrast, TFGE uses the collective talents of the team to treat the patient. Consequently, more patients can be managed effectively and a greater service is offered.

Each caregiver has a zone of responsibility around them that extends from them until the next teammate in the immediate area.

There are moments when three caregivers are in the gym with only one patient. That patient is surely being serviced while the other two caregivers are potentially documenting, preparing for their next patient, or performing some housekeeping duties within the treatment area.

Other times, when the team is really busy and a lot of patients are needing to be serviced at a particular time, the zone coverage becomes even more critical. What the zone coverage allows is a safety net cast across all patients in the building at any given time.

Basic zone coverage starts with checking your environment through observation. Verbally ask patients, "How are you doing?" and "Are you okay with that exercise?" This conveys a transfer of power to the consumer and lets the *patient* be in control. This is a more comforting and empowering communication style and a much higher perception of care.

Periodic checking in is necessary. It is the only way this system catches any dropped customer service actions. Checking in on private treatment room care—particularly on heat, ice, or machine treatment—is vital to the perception of care. Checking on a patient before they ring the service bell is a powerful service move—plus, it helps redirect any potential issues with the treatment physically. If you wait until the treatment is over to check on the patient, the patient could easily already have some complications. Check often and early!

We are looking for patients who know what is expected of them in therapy and ensuring that they appear happy and interactive. We should be checking the patients' emotional levels and communication levels readily.

If a patient does not appear happy or communicative, you must get involved immediately, regardless of whose patient it is. They are in your zone, and you are responsible for them.

If there is an issue, don't wait for the primary therapist to get involved. Fix all problems right away.

Treatment/Caregiver Skill 7: Inclusion

This is the "guest in your home" skill. According to a 2012 article in *Forbes*, "Text or Talk: Is Technology Making You Lonely," Margie Warrell reported that we are more connected than ever, yet people are reporting more isolation and depression than ever before. We should keep that in mind and avoid excluding or ignoring anyone as we work with patients, whether or not they are "our patients." Everyone is someone in The Feel-Good Experience. You want to be close to them, not smother them, and not totally ignore and forget them. The longer you leave a patient by themselves, the more they will begin to fill in their minds with questions—"What am I supposed to do next?" "Is this working, or am I actually feeling worse?" "Why isn't someone checking on me?" Those questions rarely lead to a positive service experience. Make sure your communication, instructions, and plan are clearly communicated to the patient. Repeat and ensure that everything is clear, then remain nearby to ensure any and all needs are met immediately. If a patient has to be left alone for a little longer than expected, at least have another therapist nearby to include them in the conversation they're having with their own patient. This certainly makes the time pass more enjoyably, and you eliminate the amount of time the patient will spend thinking about negative things.

Bottom line: Fill your patient's time constantly with action, movement, energy, and conversation. Rarely allow downtime or alone time, unless specifically designated in the warmup or cooldown period. It won't take long before instances of being left alone turn into complaints of poor service and even, potentially, malpractice. The act of inclusion fills the moments of isolation with connection and enjoyment.

Social events or scenes can be daunting unless you are really super confident and know a lot of people at an event. But what if you don't have confidence, you are shy, and you don't know anyone? You would still like to feel included or connected, yet no one invites you into their circle, to their table, or even acts like they care if you are there.

It's very difficult to enter into a closed group of people. If you are the one left out and perhaps would like someone to allow you in, all you need is for one person to reach out and invite you into their circle.

So, as a caregiver, if you see a patient or a teammate alone and you are nearby, it is super powerful if you engage with that person and make them feel valuable, especially in front of others.

Making people feel valued, included, popular, important, and a part of the party atmosphere *is* The Feel-Good Experience.

Treatment/Caregiver Skill 8: Getting a Serious or Withdrawn Person to Open Up

Encouraging someone to freely communicate and express themselves, particularly if it's not their natural tendency, is a very difficult task. There are some environments where we all have felt a little unsure, afraid, or uncomfortable, and thus, not willing to be vulnerable. If you don't think it's true, just consider the last wedding dance you attended. Would you have done the "chicken dance" or the "YMCA" without some "adult beverages"?

Return to the key questions on the weather and hobbies, then into specifics on them personally, on their ailment and their progress.

Somewhere within that continuum of discussion topics, you *will* get them to perk up. They most likely will not be like a dam bursting with conversation, so you will have to watch for any change in vocal tone or body language. It may be very subtle, but the cues will be there and will impress the patient that you were "in tune" with their vibes.

Once opening them up, you now have a viable communication line, and this helps with delivering optimum treatment results. Furthermore, although these types of people are difficult to read and are not open emotionally, you will certainly impact them and their perception of care. You have likely won a customer for life if you can get someone who is super quiet to open up, as they clearly feel more comfortable and connected to you.

Despite all this, remember: no level of positive communication, customer service, and psychological tricks will overcome the negatives created by an incompetent clinician. The first thing of importance is to ensure a high level of professional technical care is used. *Then*, support and strengthen that quality treatment with a high level of perceived-care customer service: The Feel-Good Experience.

Station 4: Quality Assurance/Patient Care Representative

This is performed mainly by the therapist/caregiver station, but it can be performed by anyone on the team. This station is not a true physical location like the other stations, but what's important is that it is completed after the day's session and before meeting with the scheduler before exiting the building.

"Restaurant Manager" Checks

Once care is nearing completion for the session, a patient care representative should approach the patient and perform a quality check of their satisfaction. I liken this to the restaurant manager who checks on each table to see how their meal and experience was, making adjustments as necessary. Their job is PR—to get satisfied customers to come back and to refer friends and family.

Goal Is 100 Percent Satisfaction Every Day, Guaranteed!

The mindset of the team—and, particularly, the patient care rep—is to achieve a goal of 100 percent satisfaction with every patient, every day. This requires the rep in station 4 to always be positive about the process of PT within the clinic. That can be accomplished by answering any questions and removing any barriers or frustrations that the patient may be experiencing.

These frustrations can vary from getting the time that they want on the schedule, personality conflicts, painful or uncomfortable treatment, misunderstandings in communication, poor perceived care, financial issues with insurance and billing, and referrals out to specialists. No matter the "patient situation" that is creating problems, usually the solutions are simple and just need an individual with high positivity and a strong desire to resolve and make people happy. They should go out of their way to make certain that both caregiver and patient agree to their plan of care and progress.

Patient Care Representative Skill 1: Greeting the Patient

Always greet the patient by name. This station is *only* as effective as the person's ability to know every person in the clinic. By knowing personal information about them, you have a greater chance of getting a patient to open up and refer your practice.

Simply put, you *must* have the ability to approach someone and not shy away from some potential complaints. You must be positive and prepared to handle whatever emotional state they are in. You *cannot* shrink away from them. The challenge most customer service workers have is the ability to psychologically handle complaints, bad news, or a patient venting their frustrations. Timid people who have a hard time handling conflict will opt for a comfortable interaction instead of actually seeking to hear their opinions, good or bad. If greeting or looking at someone directly is a challenge, then this station will definitely be a struggle, as it is designed to specifically inquire about problems.

Patient Care Representative Skill 2: Ask Three Questions to Ensure Quality

You must use good, strong intentions with the patient.

Ensure you are "throwing your voice" directly at them (see page 60), then recite these questions: How did your session go? How are you doing overall? Do you feel you are getting what you came to PT for?

You may have to paraphrase these questions to spark the right response from the patient or to get them to express their true feelings.

Patient Care Representative Skill 3: Handlings, Reactions, and Responding

Probably one of the most challenging skills within any customer service job is dealing with an unhappy customer.

You should be prepared to handle all comments with the appropriate emotional response and seek to "understand" the patient's situation fully. Empathy is paramount in keeping them happy. Developing a poker face is a good first step to ensure you aren't knocked off balance by any awkward comments, hyper-emotional responses, or abusive behaviors intended to manipulate.

Once you enter the scene with a neutral, unemotional mindset fixed on handling whatever is thrown at you, you can then draw up the proper emotional response.

Handling a happy patient

One might not think there is any skill needed to handle someone who is pleased. However, consider the times where you have tried to share your happiness with someone only to be met with gloom or suppression. It almost hurts twice as bad emotionally when your elation is not supported by another—thus, the importance of supporting and sharing happiness and positivity with the patient. You want to strengthen those feelings.

These happy positive moments happen when a customer is more tolerant of almost anything. They are a good time to use touch, thereby entering their physical space and using strong, positive, uplifting communication.

These are the times to encourage them to write a testimonial or a success story about their experience so that they may encourage someone else to get help and to get better. This is the time to sell The Feel-Good Experience and your organization!

Handling a disgruntled patient

According to the White House Office of Consumer Affairs, the average unhappy customer will share their negative story with at least nine other people. Those nine people each tell five more about the negative experience, and those five tell three more. If you do out the math, one negative experience can create *135 negative comments.*

Unfortunately, we live in a cynical society that demands perfection regularly, no matter how unrealistic that is. We are all strapped for time, money, and resources, and some also run short on energy and happiness. The fact that one unintended, negative experience can result in 135 negative perceptions floating around in the community is powerfully negative and damaging.

According to Colin Shaw's article, "15 Statistics That Should Change the Business World but Haven't," 13 percent of customers will tell more than twenty people about their experience. One unhappy customer can impact up to 2,100 people! Furthermore, the average unhappy customer will remember the incident for up to twenty-three years! Contrast that with the average happy customer, who will only tell three to four people about their pleasant experience, which they will only remember for eighteen months, on average.

That alone demonstrates the true power of customer service.

One of the first things you should do to handle a disgruntled patient is to get them into a private area in order to minimize collateral damage. The longer you allow a patient to verbalize their discontent openly, the more patients hear the complaints or at least feel the tension. The more tension that gets built with staff, the more likely the staff is to carry and repurpose their worries, apprehensions, or frustrations from the one disgruntled patient to the next. A raging inferno ensues, burning up all of your hard work for the day. That is why it's important to sequester the unhappy or negative patients and handle them in a vacuum.

When dealing with an unhappy customer, you must always be understanding and empathetic. Use language such as, "I understand how frustrated you must be." The art of phrasing back to them their exact emotional expression is great. They want to be heard, and they want to feel that their emotions are being supported and validated.

Next, build a partnership with them. Use language such as, "Let's put our heads together. What do you think we should do about this to fix it?" or "What would make you feel better about this?" Hitting the word "feel" triggers the psychology of exactly what the issue is: they are feeling rotten about something!

Next, give them assurances that this issue won't happen again. Then, of course, you must actually make sure that the team is aware of the issue and works to fix it, or it's a high probability you will never see that patient again.

Be sure to treat them with respect, with a lot of "Thank You," "Yes, Sir," "Yes, Ma'am," and "I appreciate you giving me a chance to make this right."

Never, never, *never* get defensive, argue, rationalize, react, use emotional words, whine, or justify the issue. The patient is the customer. The customer can go somewhere else to spend their money and get service. Your job is not to defend your team's poor actions or poorly perceived service, but to remedy it as soon as possible.

It is possible that the disagreement or problem cannot be remedied. Depending on how egregious the error was and how temperamental or objective the patient is, finding a solution could be at an impasse. When these uncorrectable patient situations do occur, you must seek a secondary win by documenting everything that transpired and ensuring that you will retrain staff so everyone on the team knows what went wrong. Tell the unhappy patient that you will take personal responsibility to ensure errors of a similar nature never happen again.

At the end of the day, with all the tasks and busywork that transpires, the final goal is to get the customer to stay with your business and to do business with you again and again. If the case is clearly one of poor service on our part and the consumer is unhappy about being charged for a poor session, then by all means, offer up a session to replace the poor one. Generally, giving away free service is not a good idea, as it never targets the core issue. Most breakdowns in customer relations are service oriented, not price oriented. Focus and correct customer service and have your entire staff determined to win over the customer.

Station 5: Front Desk/Receptionist

The patient should finish at the station they started with: the front desk and reception. This station is strictly the last stop, intended to remind, reschedule, and reconfirm in a manner that doesn't waste their time. Keep them moving, just like at station 1.

It was eye-opening, years ago, when I studied why compliance was so poor in our clinic. I found out that it had to do simply with the fact that we didn't get the patients scheduled! Instead of the problem being some deep-inner-quality issue, it really had more to do with missing people as they left the building after sessions. The number one reason patients drop off the appointment book is that they simply walked out and didn't get scheduled.

Upon installing station 5 into your service model and assertively prescheduling patients forward, you will be able to correct this trend.

Some important tools needed to ensure swiftness of traffic flow are the use of EMR software and spreadsheet tools, such as "The Patient List" proprietary tool we use in every clinic. This list captures every single patient on caseload, their prescribed visits, and duration, all right in front of the scheduler. By having this prescriptive data at the scheduler's fingertips, they can communicate on behalf of the therapist, which eliminates the need to get the therapist and confirm the plan of care.

The process being quick and assertive is the image of professionalism and effective service that most consumers appreciate. The law of delay says, "The longer the delay, the poorer the perception of service." In the end, no matter what, be accurate and keep them moving.

Station 5 Skill 1: Be Able to Face Someone Comfortably

If you can't look at someone without flinching or turning away, it is impossible to sell the fact that they need to make their next appointment. Encouragement, leading, directing, and negotiating are all a critical part of this post. It can't be done to excellence if you are too shy to look someone in the eye.

Station 5 Skill 2: Strong Intention and Enunciation When Speaking

There are some people you could be five feet away from and not know they are there, and other people may be on the other side of a large gymnasium and everyone is aware of their presence. The more confidence and self-esteem you develop, the more your attitude and personality enters the room before your body does. That is hard to quantify measurably, but is no less felt tangibly in a social environment. The greater your "aura," the stronger intention you will emit.

Building upon that principle, some can throw their voice and control a large room or an entire building from afar, even with many people around. That is the power of intention. It's the power of not yelling, but boldly and confidently speaking with the intention of being heard. At times, in our busy rehab gym, we had fifteen or more patients working in a two-thousand-square-foot area. Yet, I could still speak from the furthest distance away and have my staff hear my directives.

Those busy environments can create a lot of "noise pollution" from talking, laughter, TV, phones ringing, timers and beepers signaling treatments were done, doorbells ringing, and people on their cell phones. I liken those noisy, busy environments to headlights trying to cut through the fog when driving. You can't put on the high beams, and you can't overpower the road by speeding, but by directly, firmly, and consistently managing your speed and using low beams for headlamps, you will eventually get through the fog to your intended destination. It is done by speaking with strong vocal intention, intending to be heard.

Project your voice with an attitude. Don't mumble, keep your head up, and look the person you're speaking to in the eye, and make sure you get an acknowledgment from them that they have heard and understood you.

Station 5 Skill 3: Smiling When Speaking

Smiling when speaking brings forth the emotion necessary to modify your vocal tone and make it sound more pleasant. Adjusting body language and facial expressions redirects the other parts of our body to respond accordingly in communication, namely through our vocal tone. It's frankly impossible to frown and say "Good Morning" in a manner that is attractive and draws people to you.

A pleasant and attractive phone voice is vital to making sales and negotiating compliance if a patient wishes to cancel their appointment. So in order to be a credible communicator, ensure your body language and facial expressions match the words you are speaking, even if they can't see you. To ensure this, you can have a mirror present at the front desk when answering the phones.

Station 5 Skill 4: Planning Ahead

Competence is defined as being effective at what you are doing. The *perception* of competence is merely *looking* like you are effective at what you are doing. In order to look competent, you must plan ahead with each patient. Study names, prescriptions, and any other pertinent details that help you to best schedule them for service. Planning ahead before they leave the building preps you to be efficient and not waste their time in confirming their next appointment. Planning ahead enables station 5 to be waiting for the patient at any moment.

Again, ensure that you get an acknowledgment when confirming next appointments. It's much easier to confront and deal with the wrong date, time, or misunderstood schedule right then and there. Once the patient leaves the building, it is a game of cat and mouse to get a hold of a patient to change appointments or to track them down in the event of a no-show or cancellation.

Station 5 Skill 5: Goodbye/Salutations

This is the lasting impression on the consumer before they leave. *You must make a solid, lasting, effective connection.*

Usually, in a typical clinic, reception either doesn't say a word or perhaps might mutter a question to the patient such as, "When do you come in next?" Our schedulers are trained to *never* say, "When do you come in next?" or "When does the therapist want to see you again?" Both statements imply separate departments, not a team. Furthermore, it implies the schedulers have no authority, no leadership, and no control over their post in scheduling patients or receiving patients. It certainly doesn't relay the feeling that the receptionist is eagerly awaiting the patient's next arrival in a couple of days, because they couldn't even recall when it was they'd be back! This is a very poor customer service image and not part of The Feel-Good Experience system.

"We'll see you on Friday!" spoken with power and intention conveys competence and organization. It tells the patient we care about them and are eagerly awaiting their next visit.

This phrase is much more direct, confident, and effective at delivering The Feel-Good Experience than the common manner in which patients are treated upon leaving a clinic.

Teamwork: "Play Zone, Not Man to Man"

The Feel-Good Experience is about achieving effectiveness and efficiency by using a team-oriented approach. A team approach can treat a higher number of patients, not to mention add much more value, energy, enjoyment, and service to enhance the experience. A group of individuals is much like five separate fingers, whereas a team is more like five fingers curled into a fist, which is much stronger and resilient.

Many clinics and organizations face the challenge of taking a group of individuals and getting them to work together in true teamwork. Teamwork can sometimes be misconstrued as several individuals working in isolation, focusing on their individual tasks, but without something connecting those individuals together, they aren't a team. The connection between the many individuals within a team is an overlap of needs and wants. Each person can sacrifice their time to watch a patient of another therapist and vice versa. A caregiver who decides to clean up after their coworker because their teammate is really busy with more patients signifies true teamwork. In other words, the teammate morale is built upon each individual doing whatever is necessary as they take on the mindset that all the patients who come into the clinic are their patients also.

Within each of the five stations of service in TFGE, there are also zones of coverage, or zones of responsibility. Wherever you are as a service staff member, the area around you is your zone to cover. Obviously, at times, you will be the only person hosting or working directly with a patient and no one else is around, so you only have one patient to cover in the entire clinic. Then during other, busier times, we have to dovetail or overlap our coverage, always ensuring that no patient is left behind and everyone is getting attention.

Sometimes in sports you play "man to man," but other times you need double teams or triple teams. Help needs to come in order to cover everything.

Any patient in your zone is now your patient and your customer to service. Talking to each person and checking in on them are valid methods of service.

Covering for another therapist's patient when they need to step away for a phone call, another treatment, etc. while making the statement "Let's see what *we* need you to do next" implies a coordinated, team-oriented approach to care. In contrast, the statement "What do *you* need to do next" implies we have no clue! This is the image of very poor customer service. Always act and lead patients in a manner that says, "We know what's coming next for you, so let's check on that." That says, "We got it under control—no worries!"

TFGE promotes uniting all providers into one team.

Catching other therapists' timers on indirect treatments, completing another therapist's indirect treatment, as well as cleaning up after or before other therapists on your team all exhibit great teamwork. Those extra efforts shine through and are experienced by the patients.

High level of communication is needed in teamwork to let each of your teammates know where you will be and where you are going so your patient can be best served.

Planning steps ahead means treatment is fairly automated and removes barriers, stress, and bottlenecks.

Listening to what other team members may need around you and how to help them is critical for teamwork, as well as their listening to you.

Adaptability is the best for teamwork when it comes to covering the zones around each station. Too often, clinicians become locked into inflexible treatment paradigms. It is best practice to be flexible enough to allow another coworker to work with your patient, if needed. Systematic, automated, quality customer service that generates patterned responses can help smoothly treat a high volume of patients with very high quality.

Step up and help your teammates! We are a team, and any individual mentalities will lead to poorer quality care.

Teamwork Skill 1: Look Around and Observe "The Zone You Are In"

This skill is mindfulness, or choosing to pay attention to what is going on around you, focused totally in present time on right where you are and what you are doing. Specifically, this references being aware, peripherally, of who or what might be present in your zone. Remember the zone is the area between you and the next caregiver. Proper control for safety and service can more easily be made if all caregivers cover a zone mindfully.

Teamwork Skill 2: Finding Someone in That Zone

In building upon skill 1, skill 2 is proactively trying to find someone to influence in your zone. This can include patients, patients' family members, or even a vendor. Anyone around you.

You influence them merely by talking to them, asking questions, and granting them beingness. If you try to make anyone in your zone smile and laugh, you will be giving them great service.

The zone includes anyone, not just customers. Avoid tunnel vision when working with patients. Certainly, the goal is to focus on delivering great service and care to the direct paying customer, but do not forget about the indirect customer, as they very well could be your next customer in the future if they like how they are being treated.

Consider any vendor, FedEx driver, or plumber a potential future customer. If you seek to make the day of the mail carrier on a regular basis, you will have a greater chance of winning them. They will likely speak kindly of your practice and will certainly send any family members or friends to you, based solely on how they perceived they were treated and respected by you.

One should also observe housekeeping issues, timers/buzzers, patients, patients' family members, equipment, charts, computers, documents, and patients' activities, drills, and exercises in one's zone to ensure safe and appropriate technique.

Teamwork Skill 3: What NOT to Do in Your Zone

Remember, when you are working in the clinic, assume there are *always* eyes watching you, whether they be customers, customers' family members, other patients, or other teammates.
Others are watching to see:

- Your behavior and mannerisms.
- How you are treating your patients and those around you.
- Whether you are performing your job professionally.
- Whether you appear to be happy, competent, professional, and communicating positively.

Since others are watching, knowing what *not* to do in your zone is just as, maybe even more so, important as knowing what to do!

Things to avoid:

- Appearing bored/disinterested/disengaged
- Ignoring others around you
- Not giving immediate corrective action to
  - a patient who appears bored or unattended
  - a patient who comes to you for advice or direction. You want to always anticipate their needs ahead of time. We never want the patient leading us. We are the professionals, and in order to deliver a professional-level service that is above and beyond what they can get down the street, you must always be leading at all times.

Teamwork Skill 4: Always Look for Ways to Help

Be assertive. Set up weights and equipment for patients to ensure you are leading and directing their service.

Also, be watchful for your teammates' patients. You might need to step in and help them with a treatment, a piece of equipment, or anything else needed to assist their rehab process.

Keep things tidy once you have finished your treatment area so others don't have to clean up after you. That keeps the team moving swiftly as well as providing good teamwork.

Be willing to help cover zones when they need to step away, and then they will be more apt to cover your zones when you need to step away. This is the image of great customer service and teamwork and decreases the chances of any patient situations.

Chapter 4

Skill 3: Seek a Win-Win Outcome

A "win-win" attitude is a mindset that *must* be present daily in order for the organization to be successful. Too often a "zero-sum" outcome where someone wins and someone loses is sought in business, but in TFGE, we will not do anything unless it supports a win-win outcome for both the consumer *and* the team.

We have watched the model of PT clinics across the country and have chosen to position ourselves in alignment with other business models that work really hard at earning the trust and satisfaction of their customers. We internally handle all the phone calls, emails, and transactions for the patient's insurance, unlike a lot of clinics still demanding those actions to be done by the patient. Beyond insurance, we also seek creative packages to utilize a fair exchange of payment for their service provided if insurance coverage is not available.

We never give up on patients because we are too lazy to fight for them. Too often I hear of clinics discharging or discontinuing care for a patient who needs service simply because their insurance has denied them or they have exhausted their benefits. We have established affordable rates for when a patient has poor insurance or has been denied. We do not quit on them and always fight to carry them across the finish line if we have to, by any means necessary. It just takes a will to want to help someone and to seek a win-win outcome.

Let the Patient Determine the Win

What the patient determines as a "win" for them is what truly matters. In many cases, a patient who has dealt with a chronic ailment for decades may not believe it is feasible to achieve a 100 percent return to function, so to them, an 80 percent or 90 percent return might be a "win" for the patient. *We* do not determine their goals for them. We allow the consumer to determine their own path and their own desires for their own health. If a patient wants to throw a baseball again so he can participate in an above-forty league, we ensure that our team is prepared to do everything possible to lead him to that goal.

We do not subscribe to the ideology of insurance companies and self-limiting medical society that sets really low acceptable outcomes for patients. We don't state pessimistically acceptable or realistic outcomes for patients. I have been involved with many elderly people who were still running long-distance races, because that was their goal. I worked with farmers with multiple sclerosis who used assistive walking devices who still wanted to farm and be as active as possible in their lives. TFGE is all about the human spirit achieving greatness beyond what the world finds believable. If the patient has the willpower and the drive, we believe wholeheartedly that we should be there to lead them to what they want, hence a win-win.

Balancing the Win for Patient and Organization

We have to develop our ability to *perceive* what is really needed in every situation to ensure a win-win for both parties. It can't be a one-sided victory. If we train ourselves daily to *know* what is necessary to ensure a win for both the organization and the patient, we will be closer to achieving everyone's goals.

Customer Is Always Right but Not If It Hurts the Organization

"The customer is always right" does motivate and lead our decision making, initially. However, due to our self-respect, we *do not* support outcomes that place the customer at an advantage over the team. Keeping these scales in balance is one of the checks we use to ensure our attitudes and mindsets clearly lead us to the correct decisions.

Pro-bono and free service are *not* things we endorse as a successful business practice. Free treatment sessions or equipment are as criminally egregious to our organization as charging a patient for something they never received. One example is a criminal exchange to the organization, and the other is a criminal exchange to the patient. Both cases are unacceptable and taken very seriously in our company.

All of us like the thought of free stuff, giveaways, and handouts, but unfortunately, they are bankrupt business models. The reality is, the value of an item or service declines severely in perceived value when the price associated with it declines. Therefore, any patient who is given free service will learn to disrespect your professional service.

Additionally, the product does *not* increase in quality if we give the service away for free. Free services actually *devalue* the service and create a "lose" situation for the company. It also creates a rip-off for the next patient, who had to pay for the same service we just provided for free.

There is a reason homes, automobiles, and smartphones have a tremendous price tag on them. Physical therapy services are no different. Some PTs graduate with hundreds of thousands in school debt. They have invested a lot into learning how to best rehabilitate a patient. There is a lot of research, development investment, and cost associated with this service, not to mention the professional's need to develop high intelligence and legal protection; therefore, there should *always* be a financial value associated in exchange for PT services.

Number of Sessions and Patient's Goals

Some patients will have more or less effort, intensity, and focus from our team depending on the product or outcome they are seeking. The number of sessions, too, depends on their diagnosis, what their specific needs and wants are, and many other variables.

We never give up on patients, and intentionally always seek to ensure that a 100 percent outcome is provided to the patient/customer. Once that product or outcome is achieved, we consider the patient effectively discharged from physical therapy services. We live in the real world and know that full recovery is not possible in all cases. However, our approach to seeking 100 percent is about seeking the highest possible outcome with the highest possible practice standards. There is no value in setting your sights, goals, and values lower. In fact, when you do set lower, more comfortable targets, the consumer knows and feels it quickly. But then remember, you let the patient determine the win, and once that win is achieved **and** the organization feels they have done all they can, it is time to call it a win. Note the *and* there. The product does *not* increase in quality if we reduce sessions or stop care early assuming the patient wants to be done. To have a win-win, you can't just stop when a patient is done; it must be when both patient and the organization feel they have met their goals.

A model for determining how to negotiate a win-win is to ask a few questions of yourself, first, such as, "Have I done everything that I can for this patient, or could I extend their plan of care a little longer and get them further along in their progress?" or, "Is this person appearing more or less happy or satisfied by coming into therapy?" and, "If they are appearing less happy, what must I do to return the patient to their prior, higher satisfied state?"

Ultimately, the goal is to make the person *happy* with what we provided them by giving them exactly what they need and want in a manner in which they could easily see that *we* were the ones helping them.

The patient wants to be better by whatever means necessary, so as long as we are communicating honestly to them about time-frames and they are understanding the reality of how long it should take, they should be willing to come to sessions.

We have to be able to face the reality of all situations and read what patients and the organization need. This needs to be a dynamic, ongoing process—never ceasing!

Win-Win Outcome Skill 1: Develop a Win-Win Attitude

This skill is about recognition and positively affirming, ethical self-talk. To develop a mindset of mutual win, you have to ask yourself, "Is this truly a win-win for both the customer and the clinic?" If yes, this is the right decision. If no, then it is the wrong decision! Ultimately, do nothing unless it leads to a win-win outcome.

Win-Win Outcome Skill 2: Organizational Control

Utilizing logical organizational control can help automate by structurally establishing a win-win.

Scheduling for PT should be prescriptive, like a pharmaceutical prescription from a physician. If you want to feel better, you should take prescribed medications not as you wish, or as you feel, but as you are "prescribed." In other words, there is a proper system and structure that is proven to work.

Number of appointments

The insurance industry uses creative tactics to reduce access and limit sessions and/or treatment options. All of this comes from a "cost containment" viewpoint, yet physical therapy still remains one of the most inexpensive forms of care possible and the number one effective treatment in the improvement of lower back pain.

The insurance industry has successfully infiltrated our medical and PT schools to become the number one driver of education. It has specifically created confusion over what proper PT prescriptions are. Many believe in the insurance companies' and Medicare's approach to PT—namely, the fewer sessions, fewer treatments, and less access, the better for the patient. There is absolutely no research to support this approach. To prove it, compare a sports team who has a full-time trainer and therapist on staff. Athletes might have access to care not just one time per day, but multiple times per day. If it is not illegal to provide treatment to a sports team, and those athletes tend to respond positively to those treatments, then why is it unethical or inappropriate to allow more access for our patients?

When I came out of PT school over twenty-three years ago, I prescribed PT two times per week in a lot of cases. Every new therapist who starts out with us tends to prescribe a few visits per week. I can say definitively that if you want to make changes in the human body, it needs repetition. Whether it's getting stronger, more flexible, losing weight, or improving cardiovascular fitness, you can't achieve those physical changes with one or two sessions per week.

The thought that a patient will heal through one to two professional visits a week with the patient independently treating themselves the rest of the time is a ridiculous notion. How many people get the results they want from a coach, an accountant, or a teacher by only meeting one time per week for a few weeks? Professionals are "professionals" for a reason. They are specialists in complex areas in life and have had years and years of study and practice. One can't assume they can soak in all the value from these professionals in two one-hour sessions per week for three weeks.

We believe a more aggressive approach up front actually shortens the overall treatment time, as well as provides greater satisfaction of their experience and outcome overall. We follow the three-to-five-sessions-per-week model, aligned with a fitness exercise prescription. It takes consistent repeated stress for the body to create the necessary connective tissue changes needed to recover. I digress—bottom line, physical therapy takes time, repetition, and application of extreme effort from both therapist and patient to make the necessary changes required. Less is not more, despite what the health insurance industry might have us believe. It isn't acceptable in any other program that engages the physical body, so why is it acceptable for physical therapy? It doesn't follow logic, and it isn't good care.

Most inexperienced PTs might adjust their prescription from three times per week down to two if a patient complains of soreness, or even if they complained about having to come to therapy too often. Regardless of what is truly best for the patient's overall outcome, many of these new bleeding-heart or undisciplined therapists refuse to hold to the correct prescription. It takes a strong belief in yourself and your craft to stand tall and not yield to another's emotions. When this happens, a shift of power occurs and the patient starts leading the therapist!

This soft-sell, laid-back, go-with-the-flow mentality of yielding to consumer whims is a knee-jerk reaction and is a lose/lose scenario. No one will win in this situation. The clinician's organization loses because the patient will not get the outcome they deserve and the patient doesn't get results because the clinician is not doing what is therapeutically and professionally needed for them to get better.

These scenarios create a patient who either does not get results or gets very delayed results compared to what is possible. Furthermore, the organization will lose the benefit of a quick quality outcome and positive testimonial, plus the financial benefit of more sessions per week.

Therapist as a leader
The patient is coming to the PT as a professional, so if the therapist behaves like a strong professional, they will determine what is appropriate with non-negotiable ethics. Most of the time, when a patient states they want to quit, it has nothing to do with visits, but with their perception of service. This is a big reason why cutting prescription sessions does absolutely nothing to solve underlying service issues.

It is vital that when a patient becomes sore, disillusioned, or frustrated with their progress that the therapist spends a great deal of time explaining, in detail, their plan. Furthermore, it is crucial that the caregiver works to clear up any misunderstandings and seeks a mutual agreement with the patient about the prescription, compliance, and open communication about anything associated with their treatment—including things at home—that could affect the mutual win-win outcome.

Receptionist as a leader

Receptionists seek a win-win outcome by convincing a patient to keep their appointments. A receptionist who pays close attention to the schedule and immediately calls any patient who is five minutes late in an attempt to hold them on schedule for the day or reschedule them for a better time has been responsible for leading the patient and holding themselves and the patient accountable. Furthermore, ensuring that they always reschedule any patient who calls to cancel is keeping true to the patient's prescription requirements. A win cannot be achieved by the patient or by the organization if the patient doesn't attend their appointments. Our solution is to be very assertive with holding patients and therapists accountable to prescriptions and appointments made.

Accountability, in our setting, means firmly bringing those agreements to light. Being firm isn't a bad thing, and it is not being mean. Receptionists should not feel bad about being assertive with patients, because they are getting the patient the product they signed up to receive. Therapists need to reframe their mindset, be assertive, and ensure that patients show up. We can't deliver our product if they don't show up.

Any cases that become chronic cancellers or no-shows should be immediately handled with direct, face-to-face confrontation about their plan of care and intended results. The therapist and patient may need to reevaluate their care relationship. This meeting is not to be mean, insulting, belittling, or anything of the sort. It is literally to ensure that the patient is committed entirely, because we know our team is committed entirely. That meeting should be set to reestablish the agreement of the prescription and what is required to get better. This is merely a tough-love scenario, much like what a parent does with their kids that they love. Discipline and accountability are acts of love, because they are done out of care for the patient and all involved.

Billing manager as a leader

The billing-and-collections manager seeks a win-win outcome by ensuring everyone pays their account in full. This includes all insurance allowables and all out-of-pocket responsibilities. For patients who may have a financial hardship, payment arrangements are established. We will not be responsible for the creation of criminals who expect free services. There should be no rubber-stamp allocation on free or reduced care. Patients and patients' insurance plans *must* be held accountable for payments.

For those patients who seem to always "forget" or don't have any cash on them to pay their co-pay, the income manager should ask for a private meeting with the patient to let them know clearly what their insurance company requires and what we have to follow by law. Furthermore, they should be made aware of how many payments they have missed and what their balance is. If the patient refuses to pay their balance or shows a different side of their personality than previously seen, the red flags should go up! This individual has no intention of paying your clinic, and without a firm, face-to-face meeting, they will continue to try to get out of paying their co-pays. Any further excuse or missed co-pays should be grounds for dismissal of their care. This will obviously have to be in alignment with company policy, as well as legally appropriate. This is not to say that anyone who misses a co-pay gets terminated from care. It is merely a statement of appropriate boundaries that are necessary in running a highly ethical practice that holds both sides accountable and seeks a win-win outcome in all situations.

Chapter 5

Skill 4: Lead an Experience, Not a Transaction

I tell everyone to come here for physical therapy. It's a unique place that you can come into for health care, but it doesn't feel "medical and cold" and is very warm and friendly. My results have been amazing! The Feel-Good Experience they deliver makes you want to come back!

—Patient testimonial

O ver the course of twenty years, our rehab company has collected thousands and thousands of testimonials exactly like this. My marketing team did an extensive analysis of these testimonials and discovered common key terms patients use to describe our team in action:

- Hospitality—caring and ensuring every need is met. Coffee, conversations, treats, and they keep you entertained.
- Friendliness—conversations are very fluid and unforced. Natural and caring, doesn't feel "tight collared" like a lot of other offices.
- Technical expertise—patients are treated by multiple therapists, each with their own specialty and set of techniques, but felt like they all worked together and all helped as they were supposed to.

- Professionalism—relaxed atmosphere and approach, yet still very polished with great organization and clear leaders who were always leading and guiding.
- Wisdom—therapists and staff are young, yet behave and act like an experienced team. I felt very trusting.
- Speed of delivery—no wasted actions, everyone is quick and respects your time.
- Creative solutions—when challenges arose, they were solved.
- Clarity—patients always understood the process every step of the way and there was no sticker shock with financial obligations.
- Family-oriented—feels like you can say anything openly.
- Good atmosphere—extremely relaxed and comfortable.
- Positive influence—everyone has a great attitude.
- Passionate—passion shows through in everything they do.

As previously stated, transactional offices appear to be superior to all others and refuse to lower themselves to the level of the consumer—which is seen by the late appointment or cancellation fee, in my opinion. But transactional offices do not offer the experience needed to create good customer service.

Furthermore, any staff member who is unable to show empathy to someone who is suffering, in pain, or ill should *never* be allowed to work in a medical office of any type. The personality type that is focused solely on policy, procedure, rules, violation, and punishment is far too rigid for TFGE customer service system. They will not find job satisfaction in being flexible and creatively thinking outside the box to resolve a scheduling challenge, insurance EOB dispute, or treatment modification. Having to be on their toes is a challenge to someone who has very high strengths in exacting protocol. Creating a hierarchical system is the beginning of a systematic breakdown in health care customer service.

The belief that a doctor or PT must be straight-faced, all scientific, and spend most of their time instructing versus listening to the patient has stalled the evolution of customer service in health care. It's the culture that is broken.

According to a study in the *Journal of Medical Practice Management*, the vast majority of patient complaints about physician offices are about customer service, not specifically the doctors' or nurses' quality of care. Furthermore, the nearly unanimous consensus is that, in terms of impact on patient satisfaction, the waiting room trumps the exam room, says Ron Harman King, CEO of Vanguard.[32]

We made a conscious choice many years ago to position our company as different from other PT businesses in terms of our model of delivery. We offer every program, diagnostic treatment, and rehab known to general and orthopedic outpatient clinics. The *only* differentiator is *how* we deliver it and the attitude in which we deliver it.

We have fully embraced the fact that nearly 50 percent of all patients will get better without our laying a hand on them.[33] We reject the argument that high-quality care has to be labor intensive and complex.

We believe and have shown repeatedly in our satisfaction scores and outcomes that adding an environment that is light-hearted, positive, stress-reducing, encouraging, coaching, and which elevates a patient's dopamine responses and emotional tone is a proper healing and recovery environment. We receive anyone with open arms into our facilities, and we desire fast-paced, high-energy, high-volume environments. We *never* give up on any patients, *never* leave any patient behind, and we do *everything* within our power to drag our patients across the finish line to an outcome far greater than they ever imagined!

They may not be able to pinpoint exactly why they feel great, or why they got results quicker than with any other PT group, or why they actually look forward to coming to PT, but we know. It's because of The Feel-Good Experience.

The goal is to shoot for greatness. Be a greater patient care rep, therapist, receptionist, host/hostess, or teammate daily. Push yourself to be better and confront your own attitudes about people. Find the best in everyone. This makes success assured. Give everyone around you The Feel-Good Experience, every day!

FINAL SKILL: The Experience Is A WIN.

Any physical therapist in the world can get somebody better physically. Any physical therapist can improve a patient's range of motion or help them walk better. Any physical therapist can be friendly and nice—however, what is it that causes the mass public to be drawn to *one* particular therapist more than others? What quality is it that attracts people to a certain physical therapist's organization more than any other? The answer is the *feelings* one receives (or perceives) when one is in the presence of that therapist or that organization. They *feel good* and they have a *great experience*. Their time is pleasantly spent while with these therapists, staff members, and clinics.

Thus, if you focus only on technical treatment or technical administrative tasks, you will be disappointed. Health care is an inexact science, and it is difficult to control the outcome. The experience that the patient receives is something we can control, even when technical results are not going to be achieved. These moments give you a consolation, secondary win.

The following testimonial from a patient expresses The Feel-Good Experience in its entirety:

> *I was happy to come here and I was treated real good. Your appointments were on time, didn't have to wait. The help was real friendly. I do have a consultation with a surgeon and will definitely return here for rehab afterwards.*

This is where phenomenal customer service is a safety net to salvage the patient as a customer for life, regardless of their physical results.

Chapter 6

"What Gets Measured Gets Managed"

Ⱨow you treat people is how you will influence them. If you can effectively and positively influence someone, they are more apt to be attracted to you and your leadership. The consumer wants to be heard and felt. They want to know that their needs and wants are heard—and ultimately met—by you. It is in these moments of conflict where a customer relationship can be salvaged or destroyed. This is where strong customer service skills come in. Those "soft skills" are so important to ensure the customers' expectations are met and that a long-term relationship is developed and fostered.

What gets measured, gets managed. The relationship between a customer and the company *can* be quantitatively measured as a business-metric trend. Although relationships and emotions are not typically measurable in a logical sense, the outcome of a relationship *can* be measured and, therefore, managed. Customer service often gets misunderstood to mean simply, "being nice and friendly" or, "trying to please the customer." Unfortunately, it isn't often viewed with the mindset of a disciplined system. Shifting to this paradigm moves the unmeasurable, qualitative, emotional, relational, communicative, right-brained skillset into a left-brained, logical, measurable, quantitative business metric.

Here is our company's twenty-year annual business metric of new-customer growth, measured while using TFGE system.

Combined New Patients

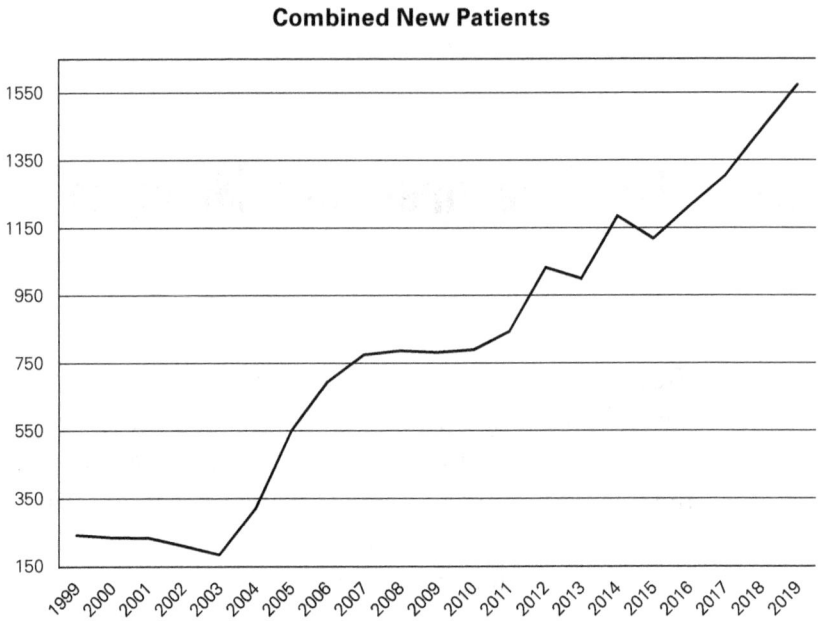

Systematically installing and performing customer service repeatedly until it becomes a culture is the key to business success. Not only do the customers get a better product and added value but the employees, team, and culture also take on a life of their own, in turn leading each of us! This brand has carried us internally as a group and as a team, emanating outwardly into our community as the "vibe" that we put out every day. It is the attitude that is palpably felt. It enters the room before we do in all situations, including marketing with physicians, doing workshops, performing health fairs, recruiting at career fairs, staff/team meetings, and patient treatment. The organization takes on the energy of the individuals and the customers and grows systemically.

Constantly serving each customer and focusing on details of their lives, communicating about their treatment, and building a relationship have enabled us to appear different from other physical therapy clinics. Our service is designed to remove hindrances, frustrations, and extra steps. Our team takes care of all the little details so the patient can simply relax, turn off their minds, destress, and enjoy what The Feel-Good Experience is all about! Growing our company over thirty-five times its size since founding and winning many awards, including Small Business of Year and Best Physical Therapy Clinic more than thirteen times in our communities, are proof of our service excellence!

It's not what we do, but *how* we do it. The product may be physical therapy services, but we feel it wouldn't matter if it were lemonade or refrigerators. The consumer demands and deserves services to be delivered with the highest quality technical skill possible, but the manner in which we *present* that technical care—by using a high level of perception of service and value to the customer, watching their happiness throughout each station, ensuring that we are engaging with everyone within our zones, seeking a win-win outcome no matter the situation, and ultimately delivering an experience and not just physical therapy services—is what makes The Feel-Good Experience a growth-oriented customer service system that captures *all* of a person.

Specific Quality Metrics

We use arrival rates (appointments-kept percentage), the percent of appointments prescheduled, and graduation percentages (including the number of success stories and number of discharged patients) to measure our success.

The little kids on the side of the street can yell out, "We have the best lemonade in town!" to every passing car, but their sales metrics have to support their claim. The best service and the best product in the world will fail without proper planning, communication,

Combined Percent Arrivals

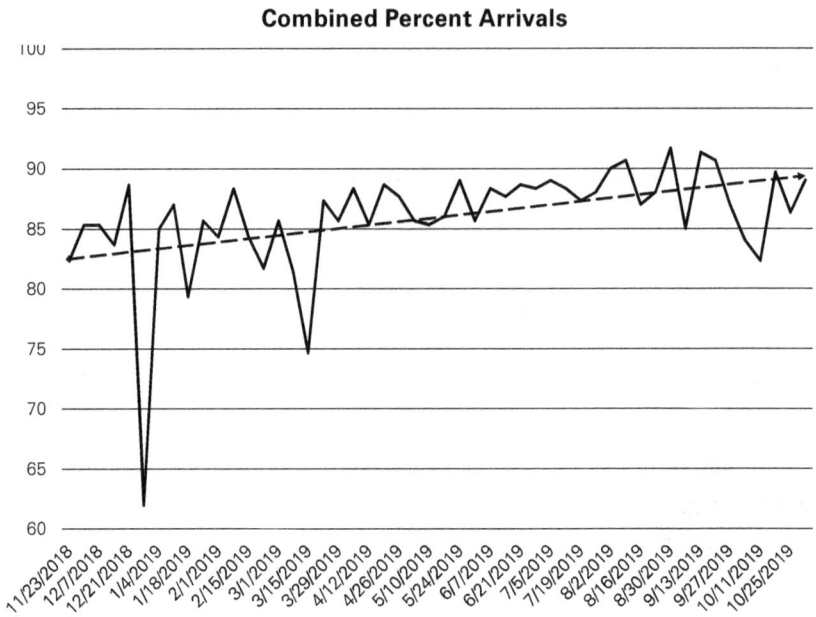

financing, delivery, quality assurance, and promotion. Taking a topic that is so feeling-oriented and subjective, such as customer service and product quality, and placing a metric value on it is the best way to prove the value of The Feel-Good Experience. Proof is in our metrics, our trends, our business growth, profitability, new jobs added, longevity of our staff, and volume of both our return business and our new business.

Our metrics manage our business, but our customers manage and direct our service trends. The customer is always right when it comes to the moving trends, tendencies, and demands the consumer places on us.

Sometimes those demands are excessive, but we can either complain about it or we can find a way to innovate and give them exactly what they demand. That mindset is the path of success in business, and the cornerstone of The Feel-Good Experience!

Our advancing, evolving, and speeding world will only move faster and faster in the upcoming years, if history is any guide. I have found it exhilarating to take an old-school, clinical, rigid, and unexciting model of health care delivery and turn it into something that mirrors a hotel or restaurant chain. There isn't one of us who would rather sit in a boring, quiet, serious environment instead of sitting at a sports bar with friends and family. The Feel-Good Experience is designed to remove all stiffness, critical details, and stressful pressures of a traditional medical office and move toward a lighthearted, easygoing, fast-moving, energetic environment that doesn't feel medical, cold, or uninviting. We want to create the desire in a person to actually *want* to come back!

They should "feel good" upon their first impression. They should "feel good" upon completing the necessary registration and insurance authorization. They should "feel good" while waiting in the reception area enjoying the coffee and conversation that are "brewing!" They should feel like a VIP upon being hosted back to the treatment area. They should feel good when receiving their pain-relieving, therapeutic treatment designed to help their body and nurture their minds. They should feel good and *know* they have been serviced. The energy from the team has been totally focused on them, and after the session is over, they should feel good knowing the front-desk receptionist knows their name, knows their prescription for care, and has them totally under control. We are meeting their every need and want, answering all questions, and removing any and all stress associated with the process of receiving PT.

That IS The Feel-Good Experience!

Notes

1 *Merriam-Webster*, s.v. "Service,"
   www.merriam-webster.com/dictionary/service.
2 Gordon W.F. Drake. *Encyclopedia Britannica*, s.v.
   "Thermodynamics," www.britannica.com/science/thermodynamics.
3 *Encyclopedia Britannica*, s.v. "Newton's laws of motion,"
   www.britannica.com/science/Newtons-laws-of-motion.
4 Mayo Clinic Staff, "Depression and anxiety: Exercise eases symptoms," Mayo Clinic, updated September 27, 2017,
   www.mayoclinic.org/diseases-conditions/depression/in-depth
   /depression-and-exercise/art-20046495.
5 "Cost of Acquiring New Customers vs. Retaining," SignalMind,
   accessed March 2021, www.signalmind.com/infographics
   /cost-acquiring-new-customers-vs-retaining.
6 Colin Shaw, "15 Statistics That Should Change the Business
   World – But Haven't," LinkedIn, updated June 4, 2013,
   www.linkedin.com/pulse/20130604134550-284615-15-statistics
   -that-should-change-the-business-world-but-haven-t.
7 Gerald Ainomugisha, "How Employee Engagement Affects
   Customer Service," The 6Q Blog (blog), accessed March 2021,
   inside.6q.io/employee-engagement-affects-customer-service/.
8 "What is DiSC," DiSC Profile, accessed March 2021,
   www.discprofile.com/.

9 "MBTI Basics," The Myers & Briggs Foundation, accessed March 2021, www.myersbriggs.org/my-mbti-personality-type/mbti-basics/.

10 "Personality test based on Jung and Briggs Myers typology," Human Metrics, accessed March 2021, www.humanmetrics.com/personality.

11 "Without a Doubt Real Colors Works," Real Colors, accessed March 2021, realcolors.org/.

12 "Transform Great Potential into Greater Performance," CliftonStrengths, *Gallup*, accessed March 2021, www.gallup.com/cliftonstrengths/en/home.aspx.

13 "Values Index," Inner Metrix, accessed March 2021, innermetrix.com/values-index/.

14 Will Kenton, "Economies of Scale," Business Essentials, *Investopedia*, updated January 17, 2021, www.investopedia.com/terms/e/economiesofscale.asp.

15 Chad Madden, "The 5 Top Trends Affecting Private Practice Physical Therapy," Breakthrough (blog), updated 2020, breakthroughptmarketing.com /5-top-trends-affecting-physical-therapy-owners/.

16 "What is DiSC," DiSC Profile, accessed March 2021, www.discprofile.com/.

17 Danny Sands, MD, "Listen to Your Patients — They're Telling You the Diagnosis!," The Doctor Weighs In, updated April 4, 2020, thedoctorweighsin.com /listen-to-your-patient-hes-telling-you-the-diagnosis/.

18 Ben Levisohn, "The Stock Market Is Always Right," The Trader, *Barron's*, updated June 7, 2020, www.barrons.com/articles /the-stock-market-is-always-right-51591404611.

19 Jeffrey Meyers, *Hemingway: A Biography* (Stuttgart, Germany: Macmillan, 1986).

20 Dr. Saul McLeod, "Maslow's Hierarchy of Needs," Simply Psychology, updated December 29, 2020, www.simplypsychology.org/maslow.html.

21 Tony Robbins, "6 Basic Needs That Make Us Tick," Behavior, *Entrepreneur*, updated December 4, 2014, www.entrepreneur.com/article/240441.

22 F. John Reh, "Pareto Principle or the 80/20 Rule," Management Skills, The Balance Careers, updated October 23, 2019, www.thebalancecareers.com /pareto-s-principle-the-80-20-rule-2275148.

23 Daniel Goleman, *Emotional Intelligence Why it Can Matter More Than IQ* (Bloomsbury, 1996), www.academia.edu/37329006 /Emotional_Intelligence_Why_it_Can_Matter_More_Than _IQ_by_Daniel_Goleman.

24 Circo Conversano, Alessandro Rotondo, Elena Lensi, et.al, "Optimism and Its Impact on Mental and Physical Well-Being," *Clinical Practice & Epidemiology in Mental Health* 6, no.1 (May 2010): 25–29, ncbi.nlm.nih.gov/pmc/articles/pmc2894461.

25 *Merriam-Webster*, s.v "Perceive," www.merriam-webster.com/dictionary/perceive.

26 "Americans' Views of Government: Low Trust, but Some Positive Performance Ratings," U.S. Politics & Party, *Pew Research Center*, updated September 14, 2020, www.pewresearch.org/politics/2020/09/14/americans-views-of -government-low-trust-but-some-positive-performance-ratings/.

27 "Physical Therapy Marketing to Generate New Patients & Grow Your Practice," Breakthrough, accessed March 2021, breakthroughptmarketing.com/.

28 "I'm OK – You're OK: Book Summary & Review," The Power Moves, accessed March 2021, thepowermoves.com/im-ok-youre-ok/.

29 "Visual Analog Scale," QuestionPro, accessed March 2021, www.questionpro.com/visual-analogue-scale-vas.html.

30 Jesal Shethna, "12 Body Language Tips for Business Meetings," Personal Development (blog), *EDUCBA*, accessed March 2021, www.educba.com/body-language-tips-for-business-meetings/.

31 "Gender Differences in Communication Styles," Public Relations and Advertising (blog), Point Park University, updated December 12, 2017, online.pointpark.edu/public-relations-and-advertising /gender-differences-communication-styles/.

32 "When Patients Complain About Docs, Care Quality Is Seldom Why," MedPage Today, updated April 28, 2016, www.medpagetoday.com/PracticeManagement /PracticeManagement/57579.

33 "Noninvasive Treatments for Low Back Pain: Current State of the Evidence," *Agency for Healthcare Research and Quality* 16, no. 17 (November 2016), effectivehealthcare.ahrq.gov/sites/default/files /pdf/back-pain-treatment_clinician.pdf.

Index

About the Author

Steve Line was born in Washington, Kansas, and grew up in a small farming community learning how to fish, hunt, and throw a curve ball at a young age. Upon graduation from high school, Steve left Kansas for the University of Nebraska—Lincoln and University of Nebraska Medical Center, where he completed his undergraduate and graduate degrees in physical therapy. He worked as a staff physical therapist for one year, then got an opportunity to open his own practice, which he has grown to twenty-six employees, three locations, and more than $4 million in valuation. Providing superior customer service and developing The Feel-Good Experience helped pave the way for business expansion.

Steve now lives in Columbus, Nebraska, with his wife, Kristine, and four children—Evan, Derek, Alexis, and Brianna. When not writing bestselling books, Steve is passionate about investments, markets, business ventures, and property and real estate management.

www.ingramcontent.com/pod-product-compliance
Lightning Source LLC
Chambersburg PA
CBHW032330210326
41518CB00041B/2049